Spontaneous
Creativity

Also by Tenzin Wangyal Rinpoche

*Awakening the Luminous Mind**

*Awakening the Sacred Body**

Healing with Form, Energy, and Light

Tibetan Sound Healing

The Tibetan Yogas of Dream and Sleep

*The True Source of Healing**

Wonders of the Natural Mind

*Available from Hay House

Please visit:

Hay House USA: www.hayhouse.com®
Hay House Australia: www.hayhouse.com.au
Hay House UK: www.hayhouse.co.uk
Hay House India: www.hayhouse.co.in

Spontaneous Creativity

Meditations for
Manifesting Your Positive Qualities

TENZIN WANGYAL RINPOCHE

Edited by Marcy Vaughn

HAY HOUSE, INC.
Carlsbad, California • New York City
London • Sydney • New Delhi

Published in the United States by: Hay House, Inc.: www.hayhouse
.com® • *Published in Australia by:* Hay House Australia Pty. Ltd.:
www.hayhouse.com.au • *Published in the United Kingdom by:* Hay
House UK, Ltd.: www.hayhouse.co.uk • *Published in India by:* Hay
House Publishers India: www.hayhouse.co.in

Cover design: Kathleen Lynch • *Interior design:* Nick C. Welch

Indexer: Joan Shapiro

Cataloging-in-Publication Data is on file at the Library of Congress

Tradepaper ISBN: 978-1-4019-5450-5
E-book ISBN: 978-1-4019-5451-2
Audiobook ISBN: 978-1-4019-5859-6

10 9 8 7 6 5 4 3 2 1

1st edition, July 2018
2nd edition, June 2022

Printed in the United States of America

A Note on the Calligraphy

The calligraphy at the start of each chapter in *Spontaneous Creativity* was created by Tenzin Wangyal Rinpoche. Each represents a fundamental principle explored in the book and is an expression of Rinpoche's joy in fully engaging these teachings with his body, speech, and mind.

For additional support in your practice, all the meditations in *Spontaneous Creativity* are available as free audio recordings. To access these recordings, please visit www.hayhouse.com/download and enter the Product ID **4895** and the Download Code **audio**. If you have any trouble accessing the meditation audio, please contact Hay House Customer Care by phone —US (800) 654-5126 or INTL CC+(760) 431-7695— or visit www.hayhouse.com/contact.

Contents

LHUNDRUP—The spontaneously perfected enlightened qualities and their effortless expression

Introduction

We are all creative. The kind of creativity I am talking about in *Spontaneous Creativity* is not just a quality possessed by the artist or a gifted few. It is a capacity we all possess, a flow of energy that arises naturally from within, enlivening every aspect of our experience. Creativity is the sacred fire that ignites positive change for ourselves, for others, and for the world. Our very nature is creative, and humankind has evolved because of this.

But it seems to be a condition of human nature, and certainly of our times, that when anything goes wrong, we disconnect from our creative nature and look around for someone or something to blame. It could be our parents, our community, our leaders, even humanity at large, but we hold forces outside ourselves responsible for messing up our lives. We may not be doing this consciously, but often we behave as if someone else is in control, making our decisions for us. We waste precious time and energy focused on others—blaming them, complaining and gossiping about them, and criticizing those who do not share our views. Instead, we need to turn our precious attention to the creative source within and take charge of our own lives.

The practices I offer in *Spontaneous Creativity* are from the dzogchen tradition of Bön Buddhism. *Dzogchen* is Tibetan for "great perfection." Perfection in this sense is not a state to which we aspire but the essential completeness we already are. The perspective of dzogchen is boundless, meaning there are no fundamental conditions or limits defining our essential nature. When we are not caught up in our pain, doubt, or fear, we can open creatively to what each moment of life has to offer and to the treasure that we have to offer life. Freed of our limitations and agendas, we become more flexible, more productive, more aware.

I have studied and practiced dzogchen since I was a young monk in India many years ago. Although the origins of these teachings lie in the ancient wisdom schools of Zhang Zhung and Tibet, their essence is like pure water. It is timeless and universal, not the province of any religion or culture. Open and inclusive, the teachings are as relevant today as they were centuries ago. Drawing on these teachings, the guided meditations and practices in *Spontaneous Creativity* are designed to help you activate your ability to meet the challenges you face and express your positive qualities in creative ways.

Chapter 1, *Connecting to the Source*, introduces you to your creative nature and reveals how to connect to the inner refuge, the sacred source of all positive qualities, such as love and joy.

Chapter 2, *Getting to Know Your True Self*, describes the medicine of the inner refuge and offers methods for accessing it through the three doors of body, speech, and mind.

Chapter 3, *A Journey from Openness to Manifestation*, maps out a five-stage path to realizing your full potential through awakening the creative powers of openness, awareness, inspiration, ripening, and manifesting. The creative potential at each stage is explored, along with practical methods for dissolving any obstacles you may encounter.

Chapter 4, *The Sacred Expression of Suffering and Wisdom*, describes another approach to manifesting your creative potential. Rushen art and tögel art enable you to clear emotional blocks and tap into your innate creativity.

In rushen art, expression of pain becomes a path to healing, while tögel art expresses the positive qualities that spontaneously arise.

Chapter 5, *Enlightened Service and Leadership*, moves beyond individual creative expression to the culmination of spiritual practice: service as a sacred path. You discover ways to apply your creative energy and innate skills for the benefit of family, workplace, community, and the wider world, expressing your natural wisdom and compassion as a caregiver and an enlightened leader.

Each of us is part of a larger family, connected to all of life in its myriad forms. If we want to go beyond simply repeating our human history, we need to do more than point out the mistakes of our ancestors. We need to embrace our personal and collective challenges with openness and courage and move forward with fresh inspiration. In this way, we will be able to receive the blessings of those who have come before us and ensure the well-being of generations to come.

My deepest wish is for you to receive great benefit from these teachings as you explore them, take them to heart, and allow them to come alive in your life.

MA—the mother, the unbounded sacred space within,
the source of all positive qualities without exception

Chapter 1

Connecting to the Source

Creativity is the food of joy. When we are creative, we express the joy of being alive. We are all creative at the core.

But what is creativity, exactly? Is it an artist toiling in her loft, a composer hunched over his piano, your grandmother icing a cake, your neighbor planting a garden? Without doubt, these are all creative endeavors. But in the Bön Buddhist tradition, creativity is far more than a display of specific skills or talents. It is an expression of our essential nature—who we truly are.

Creativity is often linked to flow—energized focus, effortless expression, total immersion in what we are doing. Both creativity and flow arise from the same source—the fundamental spaciousness of being. The essence of creativity is the spontaneous outpouring of positive qualities from that open source.

The dzogchen tradition in which I practice refers to the space of being as the mother (*ma*); to the awareness that recognizes that space as the child (*bu*); and to the union of space and awareness, mother and child, as dynamic energy (*tsal*). We are not meant to understand this relationship conceptually but to experience it personally. Every moment can be effortless, beautiful, helpful, and life changing if we are fully connected to the spaciousness of being. When we are living from that connection, qualities we associate with creative activity—joy, playfulness, humor, love, generosity—naturally arise.

Being creative is intrinsically human. Whether it is an artwork you make, a dinner you cook, or the skillful way you talk your daughter out of doing something risky, it may be creatively informed. When you are aware of the source within—the spaciousness of being that is your true nature—your actions and your expression have the potential to bring good to the world. Artistic expression—indeed, any human activity—that arises from the source is considered sacred. In my tradition, this is referred to as *trinlé*, or enlightened action. When what you express is enlightened action, it will have meaning and purpose and be of benefit to yourself and others.

Traditionally, connecting to the fundamental source of being is described as discovering an inexhaustible spring of pure water for the thirsty; the keys to the treasury of the kingdom for the impoverished; medicine for those who are ill; a home for those who wander; a best friend for the lonely; an inner refuge for those caught in samsara, the wheel of cyclic existence that binds us to suffering. Awareness of the spaciousness of being activates our creative potential. Finding ways to express it fulfills our life.

Bön Buddhism takes the view that our nature is primordially pure. So within every living being is this pure *source* of creativity, which gives rise to the positive qualities and infinite possibilities that are the *causes* of creativity. Qualities like love, compassion, joy, and equanimity are the spontaneous expression of the source and the essence of creative flow.

Creativity is our birthright, and our nature is expressive. But how do we connect with this creative energy so we can offer our unique gifts to the world? One of the most effective methods I have found for discovering creativity is through activating the creative potential of five energy centers in the body that are known as chakras. There are many chakras throughout the body; you might be familiar with traditions that focus on seven. Here, we will work with five energy centers to engage a path that begins with unbounded sacred space and continues to unfold from creative potential to creative manifestation. We will explore this in detail in Chapter 3.

Unleashing our creative energy starts with the crown chakra at the top of the head. Here we uncover the first creative potential, openness, and connect with the confidence to discover our creative potential. If we don't experience these qualities directly, we can access them through what are called the three doors: the stillness of the body, the silence of inner speech, and the spaciousness of mind. Buoyed by a sense of openness and self-confidence, we connect with the second creative potential, awareness, through the energy of the throat chakra. Here we discover our innate worthiness, which comes from connecting to our true self and feeling complete just as we are. Fears like *I can't* or *I don't deserve it*, which block creative expression, dissolve in the warmth of our attention. The third creative potential we discover is inspiration, the energy of the heart chakra. Here, we discover positive qualities like joy and love. Creativity thrives in a positive atmosphere, both nourished by and nourishing of happiness and joy, which are integral to the creative process. The fourth creative potential, which we discover through the energy of the navel chakra, is the quality of ripening. The focus here is on whatever within us or our lives is almost ready for expression and just needs a little push, a little attention from us. This is a critical place on the creative path: When a project or an idea is in this state of readiness, it can go one of two ways. If we give it the light and warmth of our attention, it can go to completion, to fulfillment. But if we withdraw our attention, it can end up in the pile of uncompleted projects and abandoned dreams. If nothing blocks our energy at this point, it takes almost no effort for the project or endeavor to complete. At the fifth chakra, the chakra of manifestation, we go the distance and bring our creative endeavors to fruition. Our creativity is no longer mere potential but is actualized in some form. Its expression can delight and serve others.

Sounds like a straightforward process, doesn't it? If only creative expression were so easy for us! There would be no problem in offering our skills and talents to the world. But people seem to find so many ways to become disconnected from their essence and the source of creativity. I knew a man who was a talented musician. Having received recognition locally, he wanted to reach out farther and spread his music around the world. He found others who could help him realize his vision. But the moment his career took off, he began to mess up. He just could not handle success, and found himself contracting back to the familiar place from which he had started as a performer. Each time he expanded beyond a certain level, deep fear surfaced and ambushed him. He felt stuck and depressed.

So how do we access our creative energy when we feel stuck? How can we rekindle inspiration? Even though we are inherently rich with positive qualities at our core, we may fail to recognize our inner resources. How do we reconnect with the source? Awareness is the key. That means knowing ourselves intimately. Knowledge of our inner essence is not acquired through formal learning. It is not the accumulation of skill or facts. It consists of recognizing openness and being aware of it in any given moment. The open source of being becomes our refuge—support that is always available to us.

Often, however, we are too busy or distracted to turn toward openness when we are searching for solutions to our problems. We get caught up in meeting deadlines, working our way through our to-do lists, and thinking about what we will do to relax when the weekend finally comes. We are so used to a low-level feeling of disconnection from ourselves and others that we might not even think the words *suffering* and *pain* apply to us. But in order to reconnect with our true nature, it is essential that we face our dissatisfaction honestly and see it for the suffering it is. The trouble is, nobody wants to be uncomfortable, so we avoid looking at our discomfort in a variety of ways. We push away negative experiences and mistake that for the power to say no. We cling to things we like and mistake that for connection. We distract ourselves by myriad clever means and call it entertainment. We are very good at avoidance.

But the path to accessing creativity and manifesting our positive qualities always comes back to openness. It is the ground, the beginning—not a step we can avoid. Since the natural openness of being is the source of creativity, whatever blocks us from experiencing a feeling of openness blocks our creativity and also our joy. In fact, it prevents all our positive qualities from arising. If you reflect on what is blocking your creativity at any given moment, you are likely to come up with a long list of obstacles: *I don't have enough time to do everything I'm supposed to do, never mind doing something creative. I'm too scattered. I have no privacy. I have bills to pay. After I get off work I don't have any energy.* There are people I know who repeat like a mantra, *I can't do it. I can't do it. I can't do it.* Send yourself a message like that often enough, and creativity doesn't stand a chance!

There are so many possible blocks to living creatively, so many excuses for not taking action. Resolve one block and clear it off your list, and chances are you will find another to replace it. Our lists are never-ending in this way. But the items on our lists are not the problem. The question to ask is not *what* is blocking you but *who. Who is the one who is suffering?* How you experience yourself, the identity you create, is the number-one block to accessing the source of creativity within. Holding on to the sense of an *I* that is fixed and solid—and will be with you always—is one of the fundamental errors identified in the Bön and Buddhist traditions. We suffer not because of what is happening to us, but because of this *I* we identify with and cling to so tenaciously. This is the cause of our suffering. There is a way out, however. Through meditation practice we can look inward and explore the fixed *I* who suffers. When we do that, we come to see that this sense of *I* can only continue to exist because we maintain it with our thoughts and imagination. When we stop building up *I* in this way, it loosens its grip. We begin to feel a sense of openness. That narrowly focused self no longer controls our thoughts, no longer blocks access to inner space, to the creative source.

The hitch is that this false *I* is often hidden, driving our reactivity from just beneath our awareness. We are so used to identifying with it that we act as if it is real. When we expose this *I*, we may react with attachment or aversion, either clinging to it, unable to imagine life without it, or searching for ways to get rid of it. The world is full of well-meaning advice on self-improvement, and many people meditate in an attempt to replace the undesirable self with another, more positive self. But those efforts are fruitless and miss the point. The fundamental issue that is not being addressed is holding on to the ego's insistence that we have a solid, unchanging identity. Discovering the truth of egolessness or selflessness is a core teaching in my tradition and an essential step on the path to manifesting our positive qualities.

Rather than bypassing or avoiding pain or trying to get rid of it, we need to open fully to our pain and discomfort. Whatever form this *I* takes—and it can be as changeable as your mood—it is, without doubt, pain of some sort. I call this a *pain identity*. Perhaps you meet the *I* who is insecure, uncertain, or afraid to be noticed. Perhaps you are carrying around an *I* who isn't getting the recognition she deserves. Whether your fear or insecurity appears as a critical voice or a pervasive feeling of unhappiness, it has probably lived with you for a long time. But if you recognize pain—even entrenched pain—directly, your attention will have the force of an acupuncture needle hitting precisely the right point to release blocked energy. A moment of fear or insecurity, properly encountered, can lead you to the discovery of your true nature.

To bring your awareness to a painful experience, pay attention to the feelings in your body, the emotions that are arising, the thoughts that are coming to mind. Touch your experience directly with unbiased awareness as you open to it. Don't move away from any part of your experience. Show up. Be there. Don't abandon yourself or your discomfort.

I often suggest treating pain or fear as you would treat a close friend who came to you fearful and trembling. What would you do? You would be fully open to that person, right? You would not divide your attention at that moment, cell phone in hand, and say, "Oh, wait a minute, I'm getting a text. But go ahead. I'm still listening." No, you would focus your full attention on your friend. You would *be* there for her. When you are fully present to someone's pain, a deep sense of caring and warmth naturally emerges. It is the same with your own discomfort. If you are fully present with it, it will begin to shift. As the pain releases, warmth spontaneously arises from the space of being.

TSAL—The dynamic energy that arises spontaneously
from the union of openness and awareness

Chapter 2

Getting to Know Your True Self

Our essence is changeless. There is nothing to change, nothing broken that needs fixing, nothing we need to improve upon. We are fundamentally complete as we are. *Perfect*, as the texts describe it. Perfect in this sense refers to the teaching in Buddhism that we already have all the enlightened qualities within us. But even though we have this perfected nature, we don't always realize it or draw on it in our lives. We all recognize kindness and have the ability to be kind, but often we are not kind. We recognize the warmth of a smile, but often we are not smiling. Much of the time what we express in life is not inspired or warm but driven by what are called the three poisons: aversion, desire, and ignorance. We push away or avoid what we don't like; that's aversion. We want more of what we like; that's desire. And we are unaware of our true nature as open and perfected beings; that's ignorance. Being unaware of our true nature is the root cause of suffering. The pain, the dissatisfaction, that dogs us through life is the pain of disconnection—being disconnected from our fundamental goodness, from the infinite possibilities and positive qualities that arise from the source within.

Formal meditation supports us in connecting with the open source within and living from that source. Throughout this chapter there are meditations to help you connect with the source of creativity and a detailed map for discovering your creative potential and unleashing your creative energy. But before you embark on this journey, I want to emphasize that although *Spontaneous Creativity* contains formal meditation instructions, sitting on a cushion on the floor with your legs crossed is not the only way to practice. The purpose of meditation is to connect us with the sacred ground of being, and there are many ways to make that connection. For a musician, playing an instrument can be a meditation. For someone who loves to cook, preparing a meal can be a sacred practice. Any activity can be a meditation if you are connected to the spaciousness of being—the source—when you give it a voice or form.

The positive results experienced from connecting to the source are so great that you might find it hard to trust that there is a single medicine that can relieve your suffering. But there is. Awareness of the openness of being is that single medicine. But even if you have tasted the medicine, connected with your open nature, felt the creative spark of connection, maybe even transformed a painful relationship to someone or something—a bad habit, perhaps—you might still be wondering how connecting to inner space with awareness can serve you in every moment. As with any teaching or practice, it is important to explore this for yourself. Test the power of open awareness in all aspects of your life. See what happens, what is transformed. As you taste the fruits of your practice, you will come to see life as an adventure and a gift, and you will be moved to express the joy of living creatively in beneficial ways.

Practicing formal meditation

Meditation connects you with the source of infinite creativity. It is your support for overcoming obstacles and becoming familiar with the positive qualities of your true nature, from which you express your life fully. The recommendation is to meditate at the start of your day so that you can experience the benefits throughout the rest of the day. In the beginning, short, focused practice periods are best. Gradually, you will be able to increase the length of your meditation period if you choose to.

The Five-Point Posture

In formal meditation, whether you are sitting in a chair or on a cushion on the floor, the position of your body is an important support for experiencing open awareness. The traditional meditation position is called the five-point posture.

- **Sit cross-legged on a mat or cushion.** This contains your energy and keeps the core of your body warm.

- **Keep your spine straight.** This allows your breath to flow more naturally.

- **Keep your chest open.** This supports an open-hearted connection to your experience.

- **Rest your hands in your lap,** four finger widths below the navel. Place the hands in the position of equanimity or equipoise as a reminder that your meditation is a balance of openness and awareness. Bring the tips of the thumbs to the base of the ring fingers. With palms up, rest the fingers of your left hand lightly on the fingers of your right hand.

- **Keep your head erect** and tuck your chin slightly to elongate the back of the neck. This helps to cut the incessant stream of thoughts.

Your eyes should be open and receptive, gazing downward slightly to minimize distractions.

If you cannot sit comfortably on a cushion, you may sit in a chair. Sit up straight, without leaning against the back of the chair. Rest your feet on the floor.

Meditation practice should never be forced. You want it to be spontaneous and fresh. But in the beginning of your practice, you will need to use some effort to capture your moving mind by focusing it. In the meditations that follow, you will explore placing your focus first on the stillness of the body, then on the silence of speech, and finally on the spaciousness of the mind—the three doors. As your attention rests on the object of focus and you feel its support, the tendency of the mind to wander will lessen. With the support of the focus, the restless mind is tamed. As your moving mind begins to rest, you are less distracted by thoughts and inner dialogue. The true nature of the mind is open, and your focus supports you in recognizing this spaciousness. Your practice then is to rest in openness itself. No matter what arises—thoughts, feelings, sensations, recollections—the instruction is the same: *Leave it as it is.* Be aware of the spaciousness of mind that allows everything to arise, dwell, and then dissolve.

The door of the body

To explore the door of the body, begin by reflecting on all the movement you have expressed through your body over the years, all the physical effort you have expended. Think of all the stairs you have climbed, the snow you have shoveled, the leaves you have raked, the counters you have wiped. Take a thorough inventory of all the repetitive activities like this in your life, past and present. Notice any underlying dissatisfaction reflected in those movements. Consider something you had to put a lot of physical effort into that you no longer want to do. Can you release any impulse to pursue it? Allow time for this reflection. The purpose of it is to support you in recognizing the opportunity this moment offers you to rest in stillness. Receive it as a gift.

Accessing stillness through the door of the body allows you to experience your changeless essence. The first step is to stop moving and rest your attention on your body. Become aware of being still. The stillness of your body becomes the support for your moving mind to rest. We may think that letting the mind wander all over the place is giving it freedom. But we are unaware that what is actually driving this restless moving mind is our unacknowledged dissatisfaction. This movement expresses the pain of disconnection from the source within. The mind that wanders, searching, will never find permanent satisfaction. So in meditation, we let that mind rest.

Resting your awareness on the stillness of your body does not guarantee that all thoughts or sensations will stop arising. They will still arise, but following your thoughts or elaborating on them will cease to interest you. As you continue to sit, you will connect with the stillness of being. Experiencing the stillness of being includes your body but is not limited to the body. You discover a sense of being that is unbounded—a sense of all-pervasive spaciousness. The door of stillness of the body opens you to this genuine refuge, the space of being in which we are all connected.

Meditation:
Stillness of the body

Take a comfortable position with your spine upright and chest open. Bring your attention to the stillness of your body. You are not simply being still; you are being aware of the stillness.

Rest in that stillness. Be that stillness.

As you rest in stillness, your mind may move, captured by thoughts, feelings, sensations, recollections. As you become aware that you have lost connection with the stillness, simply bring your mind back to the stillness in your body. Reconnect and rest.

Gradually become aware of the stillness of being. This sense of being includes the body and yet is not bound by the body. Let this expanding awareness support you.

Recognize this sense of openness, of spaciousness that is unbounded. Rest here. This unbounded space is sacred. This is the space in which we all are connected. This space is referred to as the mother, the base, the ground of all. Rest in the space as a child rests in the lap of its loving mother—safe, secure, comfortable, loved. Release fully into that space. This space is ageless, changeless, boundaryless, free from all limitations. Become the space.

Trust this unchanging space of being, this refuge. Rest here as long as your experience is fresh.

Dedicate the merit of your practice with the aspiration: *In liberating my own being, may I benefit others.*

For those who fear change, as you turn your awareness to the inner refuge, your fear will release and you will find protection. For those who feel lost, as you turn your direction to this sacred inner space, you will find your way home. For those feeling isolated and lonely and needing connection, as you turn your gaze to this inner sacred space, you can feel a connection to the universal mother. Whatever suffering you experience, bring it to this space of being. Allow it, feel it, let it release in this space. Feel the ease that comes from resting here. This is a taste of inner freedom.

The door of speech

Another way to enter the inner refuge of your true nature is through the door of speech. You can explore this door too through reflection and meditation. Begin by thinking of all the effort you have expended in your life on speaking, voicing your opinion, being heard, being acknowledged. Conversely, think of the effort you have made to silence yourself in order to avoid feeling embarrassment or shame. Consider the energy you have expended in gossiping, blaming, and criticizing yourself or others. Can you allow all this effort to release? Can you give your voice permission to rest? Recognize this opportunity to rest in silence as a gift. Receive it fully in this moment.

The door of the silence of speech brings you to awareness of being, awareness that is fresh, uncontrived, and illuminating. You enter this door by listening to the silence, then hearing it, then feeling it, and then becoming the silence. Begin by being quiet and listening to the silence. Notice your tendency to follow sound, including the sound of your own inner dialogue. As you shift your attention to the silence, it will support you in releasing your reactivity to inner and outer sound. Let silence support you in releasing the tendency to talk to yourself, to comment on and describe and categorize your experience. Release the tendency to criticize or judge. As you rest in silence, the energy that goes into reactivity is released and becomes available for more creative use. Silence is like an ocean, deep and vast. Sounds are the waves, currents, and ripples in the ocean. Can you rest in the ocean of silence, letting the sounds within and around you just be?

When the noise of your inner dialogue no longer distracts you, awareness emerges that is not wedded to your thinking mind. It is naked of opinion. This awareness is fresh and vivid and alive in the moment. It is not the result of effort; it is spontaneous. The texts describe this awareness as illumination—a sense of knowing your essence.

The door of the silence of speech opens you to pure awareness of the sacred space of being.

Meditation: Silence of inner speech

Take a comfortable position with your spine upright and your chest open. Bring your attention to the silence within and around you. You are not simply being silent; you are aware of the silence.

If you have a tendency toward inner dialogue, you will need to use effort to listen to the silence.

As you begin to hear and feel the silence within, you can release the effort of listening and simply rest in the silence. Allow the silence to hold you. When you stop talking to yourself, you will feel a sense of peace.

As you rest supported by silence, awareness spontaneously emerges. This is awareness that discovers the unlimited potential in openness.

Rest here as long as your experience is fresh.

Dedicate the merit of your practice with the aspiration: *In liberating my own being, may I benefit others.*

Discovering pure awareness is like the experience of someone struggling in poverty who suddenly discovers she is of royal birth and has inherited the treasury of a kingdom. Awareness that discovers the unbounded spaciousness of being is the key to your inner treasury. You feel full and complete as you are in the moment. Nothing is missing. You feel worthy. As you connect with this awareness, you taste the infinite potential of your being. This awareness is a refuge that is always available to you.

The door of the mind

The third door to recognizing your inner essence is the door of the mind. To enter this door, reflect on the considerable effort you have expended in your life on learning and remembering. You have studied facts and numbers and names and connections and patterns to try to make sense of life—to understand, find order, memorize, do the right thing, be smart, be correct, gain approval, win. Who hasn't imagined a better life, a way out, a way in, a way to the heart, a way to escape? Take time to reflect on the accumulation of all this mental effort. The purpose of this reflection is to support you in connecting with the natural warmth of presence, which is often obscured by thinking. Let that mental effort release now. Receive the gift of resting the moving mind. Let the wind of your thoughts exhaust in the open sky of your mind.

We usually think of the mind as the faculty that allows us to think and reason and imagine. But in meditation, we draw our attention to the spaciousness of the mind. This spaciousness is vaster than any thoughts or sensations or emotions or recollections moving through it. Spaciousness has no color or shape or boundary, and the mind that seeks and searches can let go of any effort and rest here. The search has ended. You are home, and you are present. You don't need your thoughts to know that you are present.

Awareness, naked of the clothing of the conceptual mind, is like the sun shining in a cloudless sky. In this space of being you experience the warmth of presence. As you abide here, this natural warmth gives you a fundamental sense of well-being, goodness, and joy.

Meditation:
Spaciousness of mind

Take a comfortable position with your spine upright and your chest open. Bring your attention to the space in and around your heart. Release any effort and rest here.

Continue to open your focus and rest in openness. When you notice your focus narrowing on a thought or an image or a sensation, open it. Without suppressing or following your thoughts, let them be.

Feel the spaciousness of being. Rest here.

Awareness is like sunlight in the open sky of your being. As you abide in open awareness, feel the natural warmth.

Rest here as long as your experience is fresh.

Dedicate the merit of your practice with the aspiration: *In liberating my own being, may I benefit others.*

In the spaciousness of being and the light of awareness, you merge with the natural warmth of presence. You become one with the warmth, and in that oneness feel safe. This is the warmth of positive qualities, of love, compassion, joy, and equanimity. These positive qualities are all available to you, and they emerge spontaneously. The door of the spaciousness of mind opens you to unlimited positive qualities. This is the third aspect of the inner refuge. Expressing these qualities fulfills your life and benefits others.

When you sit down to meditate, empty your body of the impulse to move, empty your speech of the urge to comment, empty your thoughts of the need to improve.

Simply be in stillness, silence, and spaciousness with awareness. When you rest the moving, searching mind, you come home to your true nature. By being aware of the stillness of the body, the silence of speech, and the spaciousness of the mind you connect with the three qualities of the inner refuge: the unbounded spaciousness of being, pure awareness, and the warmth of positive qualities. Each time you meditate you become more familiar with this inner refuge.

The medicine of the inner refuge

Being introduced to the inner refuge of the natural mind sets in motion a powerful journey of transformation. Ignorance of the inner refuge—our true nature—is the root cause of suffering. We are not trying to get ignorance to change. But ignorance needs a good rest, because it has been working too hard. It is inefficient and unproductive and drains our energy with no positive outcome. When we are not aware of the openness of being, we suffer, and we try to do anything to relieve our discomfort. We look for things to be different from what is here. Misguidedly, we often seek refuge—some semblance of stillness, silence, and spaciousness—by changing our circumstances, our mood, even our thoughts. But these actions are driven by the three poisons—aversion, desire, and ignorance— and cannot free us from suffering. We need to connect with the openness of our being, not disconnect from it. We need to be conscious, not unconscious. We need to allow our experiences, not run away from them. We need to know rather than wander in the unknown. The direct root to the awareness of openness that is the source of creativity is to allow the restless moving mind to rest. As always, the instruction is: *Leave it as it is.*

Spontaneous creativity arises from being fully conscious and living connected to the source, the inner refuge. When we are connected, the three attributes of the inner refuge—unbounded spaciousness, pure awareness, the warmth of positive qualities—become available to us. Each attribute has a distinct function in clearing the obstacles to the full expression of our positive qualities.

Unbounded spaciousness

Resting in the space of being clears obstacles. Often, however, we don't trust that. You may worry *If I allow my fear to fully emerge, if I don't try to control it, won't it take me over?* But as great as your fear is, it is nowhere near as vast as the spaciousness of being. When you experience fear, instead of shutting down or constricting in any way, open to it. If you keep fear at a distance, it will have power over you. But if you stop pushing it away—ignoring it or trying to suppress it—the power of openness becomes available to you. The fear dissolves because there is no inherent power in it. It is a construct of your mind; therefore it can deconstruct. That's all there is to fear.

If you are connected to the space of being, everything you experience is workable. The space of being is always unbounded, but whatever moves within it has a bounded sense of itself. Therefore, when you are connected to the space of being, obstacles will dissolve, simply because an obstacle cannot remain unless it is being maintained. If you are secretly maintaining something—feeding an obstacle—that effort will be exposed, allowing you to release your effort and rest in the openness itself. What appears is not permanent. If you are resting in openness, you are not feeding your fear, so it exhausts itself. Connecting with the space of being clears obstacles. They self-arise and self-liberate. This is why the openness of your being is a true refuge from suffering.

Pure awareness

When what you are focusing on, such as your fear, is met with open awareness, it dissolves. But what happens then to the self, the *I* who was experiencing the fear? If you bring naked attention to the self, it too releases. What is left is awareness that directly experiences the space of being. Then what happens? Your energy starts to move. Thoughts and ideas are not solid and fixed, and they re-arrange themselves in fresh and inspired ways. So much freedom becomes available to you! As you rest in the openness of being, old habits dissolve, allowing for the emergence of new possibilities. Pure awareness is a true refuge that liberates suffering.

The warmth of positive qualities

Awareness that is not wedded to thoughts and opin-ions but directly perceives the openness of being ignites the warmth of genuine presence. Qualities like joy and love emerge. The warmth of these positive qualities is the third attribute of the inner refuge. Warmth expands and moves us to express creatively. A fresh thought arises and guides us in a new direction. Something is happening! Windows are opening! Appreciate this alive-ness. You might feel inspired to write, to paint, to cook, to reach out to people. Acknowledge and celebrate your creative expression. The warmth of positive qualities is a true refuge that heals your suffering and benefits others.

The three precious pills

As much as we might want to stay connected to the inner refuge, we often disconnect from it. So, how can we reconnect to the source? Before we can reconnect, we need to recognize the ways in which we disconnect. I refer to this state of disconnection from the source as a pain identity. It is composed of a pain body, pain speech, and pain mind.

A pain body is any sense of *I* that is solidly identified with a state of mind, a feeling, an opinion, or a reaction: *I am afraid; I am in pain; I am stuck; I don't like this; I have to figure this out.* In contrast to the openness that allows all experiences, when we experience ourselves as a fixed and solid sense of *I*, we are contracting—limiting or blocking the potential inherent in any given moment. Pain speech refers to the constant inner dialogue of judgment toward self or others. Much of the time our inner dialogue is not fully conscious, but it obscures our basic confidence and sense of worth. Pain mind is the imagination of fear. When fear drives the mind, it imagines all sorts of dire possibilities that may or may not happen. So many of the images that fear creates drain our energy and block inspiration. In fact, any of the three—pain body, pain speech, or pain mind—can drain us and block our creativity.

The seemingly solid experience of *I* is not who we fundamentally are, but often it is who we experience ourselves to be. The good news is that we are not as fixed or solid as that *I* appears to be. Even a glimpse of the inner freedom arising from the openness, clarity, and warmth of the natural mind ignites us. Then we realize that fundamentally, we are not our thoughts, moods, anxieties, and fears. There is so much more to life than what the conceptual mind grasps.

There are three prescriptions to liberate us from this limited sense of self. I call them the three precious pills. A pill is medicine, and in this case the medicine is the instruction for where to turn and rest your attention when you need healing. The first instruction is to bring your attention to the stillness of your body. I refer to this as taking a white precious pill. Bringing attention to the silence of your speech is taking a red precious pill. And bringing attention to the spaciousness of your mind is taking a blue precious pill. The colors of the three precious pills derive from Tibetan Bön visualization practices. We connect to the sacred body through white light, to sacred speech through red light, and to sacred mind through blue light.

Taking the precious pill of the body means focusing on the stillness of your body and resting your attention there until you experience a glimpse of the inner sacred space of being. Taking the precious pill of speech means focusing on the silence of your inner speech and resting your attention there until you experience a glimpse of awareness that is fresh and vivid and free. Taking the precious pill of the mind means drawing your attention to the space in and around your heart and focusing there, without suppressing or following your thoughts, until you feel the warmth of being.

These three precious pills are the medicine that allows you to access the source of inspiration and positive action at any moment of your life.

The white precious pill: liberating the pain body

Perhaps you dread going to work every day but you have no choice. Instead of pushing yourself out the door while imagining the relief you will feel on the weekend, just stop and be conscious of exactly what you are experiencing. *I have so much to do today; I have no energy; I can't stand my boss.* Take a deep breath. As you slowly exhale, connect with your body and feel the stillness of your body in this moment. Rest your attention here. Let the experience of stillness support you in feeling more connected to yourself. As the energy you invested in disliking or avoiding your experience begins to release, you get a glimpse of openness. There is healing in that openness. You might experience the shift from distress to relief immediately but then find that your distress returns later. When you notice that again you feel distressed, recognize it without judgment and take another white precious pill: Stop and connect with the stillness. Feel the stillness of your body. Take one deep, nourishing breath and again feel the relief of spaciousness.

This is a practice you can repeat as often as needed throughout your day. It is not simply a means of relaxing your body or releasing tension in your belly, although that may occur. Whenever you recognize that your pain identity is blocking the open space of your being, you can remedy this with the white precious pill. It is important to repeat this short practice until you recognize that your pain identity—the one who is suffering, the one who is blocked—is not permanent or fixed, and you have the confidence to meet it fully and discover opportunities that you were previously unaware of.

The red precious pill: liberating pain speech

Just as the white precious pill liberates the suffering of the pain body, the red precious pill liberates the suffering of pain speech. Have you ever heard yourself saying things like, *I'm having such a bad day. What's wrong with me? I can't believe I forgot that.* These voices of anxiety and self-criticism are so familiar that we begin to believe in the reality they portray. They literally bind us to a certain version of reality in the moment. When you realize you are talking to yourself in this way, stop. Take a deep breath, and as you slowly release it, listen to the silence that is within and around you. Begin to hear it. Regardless of how noisy the internal or external environment is, silence is always available. Hear it, feel it, rest in it. This instruction is not about spacing out or avoiding your experience but about being fully present in the moment without following your inner dialogue. Let these inner voices be as they are without following them or arguing with them. As you listen to the silence, gradually you may experience a sense of relief, a sense of freshness. Playfulness and humor may spontaneously arise. You will realize that there is more support available to you in the openness of being than from the incessant chatter of the voice in your head.

The blue precious pill: liberating pain imagination

The blue precious pill liberates the suffering of pain imagination. Have you ever had the experience of waiting for the results of a medical test? You probably had rapidly shifting scenarios coursing through your imagination, positing certain results and projecting the actions you would have to take with each one. In an instant you could feel your anxiety rising to meet the visions that took over your mind. Often we try to counter the pain imagination with another more positive vision: *Look on the bright side. See the glass as half full.* But have you ever considered that there is a fundamental openness available that does not carry the bias of either hope or fear? Openness is like the vast sky. No matter what is happening in the sky, the sky remains open. The sky is not arguing with what is appearing in it. So when thoughts and visions arise in your mind, bring your attention to your heart and take a deep breath. As you slowly release the breath, open to the space in and around your heart, the inner sky of being. Let this sense of sky within and around you hold you and all the movements of your mind. If you are not feeding your thoughts with more thoughts, they cannot remain as they are. They will exhaust themselves. As you become aware of openness, release into it. You will feel a genuine sense of well-being as you are held in openness.

DZA—The seed syllable of spontaneous and
creative virtuous action

Chapter 3

A Journey from Openness to Manifestation

The glimpse of openness that the three precious pills gives you, no matter how fleeting, reveals the truth of your being. Fundamentally, you are whole, and you can realize this and live your life from this realization. To do so, however, you need to be willing to work with yourself moment by moment, to release the tyranny of your pain identities so you can experience each moment directly. Supported by the three precious pills, you discover that what may begin as merely a glimpse of openness becomes a reliable experience of it.

Whenever we try to move from here to there in life, having a map can be useful. How many of us now rely on the GPS app on our cell phones to get to new and unfamiliar places in a timely way. But there is also an internal map or guidance system to help us move from pain to freedom, from feeling blocked to feeling open and expressive—a map that helps us discover the hidden treasure of our aspirations and visions, and bring forth our gifts in this lifetime. If you want to live a more conscious life and express your gifts before you die, consider what those who have gone before you have relied on for spiritual guidance: an energetic navigation system that is inherent. Through this energetic navigation system you can find the inner refuge at any given moment, no matter what is appearing in your life or what obstacles you encounter. Developing a relation to this energetic system allows you to recognize and meet obstacles and challenges, and then reconnect with your positive qualities, so you can express yourself fully in beneficial ways.

The energetic navigation system or map I am referring to relies on five energy centers in the body. Each center is what is known as a chakra, a Sanskrit word that literally means wheel—in this case a wheel of light. Each of the chakras in the system has a specific location in the body. To use the map, you rest your attention at each chakra and abide there in open awareness. In abiding—resting your attention in open awareness—you clear any energetic blockages and activate the wisdom qualities of that chakra.

Each of the five energy centers has a corresponding syllable or sound that serves as a seed, a living symbol of the wisdom qualities available at that location. The five syllables and their corresponding chakras are:

- *A* (pronounced *ah*): Crown of the head

- *OM* (rhymes with *home*): Throat center

- *HUNG* (the vowel is pronounced *oo* as in *hook*): Heart center

- *RAM* (the vowel is *ah*): Navel center

- *DZA* (a fricative sound *dz* or *ts* and then *ah*): Secret center, four finger-widths below the navel

Each syllable represents a power to transform our confusion or limitations and bring forth our positive qualities. *A* represents the power of openness; *OM*, the power of awareness; *HUNG*, the power of creative inspiration; *RAM*, the power of ripening; *DZA*, the power of manifesting.

In the pages that follow, we will explore this energetic map, chakra by chakra, as it guides us in recognizing who we truly are and manifesting our positive qualities.

A ~ THE POWER OF OPENNESS

If we ask ourselves honestly if we have appreciated the gift of this life and expressed as fully as possible what we have to offer, many of us will feel that we have fallen short of our potential. The older we get, the more we may focus on missed opportunities or regrets. As we age and adapt to the demands of day-to-day life, we tell ourselves that it is only natural for our creative fire to dim and that the energy to innovate and effect change is for the young and enthusiastic. The truth is, we may fear change at any age and commit much of our energy to being safe and comfortable rather than going beyond our habitual tendencies in order to discover openness. But recognizing the openness of our being is the essential first step of the creative process.

How can we work with our need to be secure without shutting down our capacity to reach out and explore and discover the power of openness? Any creative journey begins with an open screen, an empty canvas, a blank sheet of paper, silence, an unformed moment. So the question becomes, what is your relationship to this unformed moment? Do you feel fear or uncertainty? According to the teachings, the experience of openness, when recognized, is the source, the mother who gives birth to all that arises.

It is easy to enjoy the spacious experience of looking out at the horizon when we are near the ocean, or stopping to admire the panoramic view from the highway when we are on a road trip. But how do we feel when we encounter silence in the midst of a conversation with a friend or at the side of a loved one who is ill and unable to communicate? What happens when we find ourselves staring at the blank computer screen before composing our thoughts for an important e-mail? How do we react to the space that opens up within us when we lose our train of thought? Or our beloved pet? Or our aging parent?

Often the inner space we perceive is announced by loss and then occupied by our nervousness, uncertainty, anger, or lack of confidence. We frequently respond to discomfort with aversion. But we can choose a different view. We can release the energy that goes into aversion and see loss as an opportunity—a doorway to the openness of being. The first refuge is to connect with the unbounded space of being. Connecting with the space of being is also the first step in expressing creatively. The refuge is discovered within. But if you close your eyes and look within yourself, very often you become aware of internal chatter or discomfort. You identify with the discomfort because it is so familiar. Then, with the thought *I am uncomfortable*, you get stuck.

It's Monday morning, and you are slipping into your professional pain body as you drive to work. Is there any sense of unboundedness there? Yes, if you are aware in the moment. You might realize, *Whew, I don't have to drive this way—gripping the wheel, leaning forward, tightening my stomach. I don't have to obsess over the day to come. I can bring my attention to stillness and begin to feel some shift in my consciousness.* Simply through being aware and taking a few breaths, something opens up. You can shift from a bounded, painful space to an unbounded, open space. Let's say it's Monday morning again, and this time you don't have a job. You need a job, and it is painful not to have one. As you experience anxiety, if you bring your attention to stillness, your experience will shift. Whatever the scenario, your thoughts about it can obscure the openness of being that is always available to you. Stillness gives you access to openness.

In the teachings of dzogchen, it is said that through thought we will never understand the truth. No matter how smart the conceptual mind is, it can never grasp the truth of being. Access to the source is not through thought but through nonconceptual, naked awareness. It is not about looking at the sky and *thinking* about what is right for your life at this time. It is about drawing your attention to the sky and letting it rest there for 15 minutes. The sky will give you more answers than any thoughts could. Resting your mind on that simple support—the openness of the sky—will bring more clarity than repeating *What should I do?* over and over again.

The path to being yourself and knowing yourself and creatively expressing your gifts begins with openness. You can begin at any moment, as this open space of being is always here, always available. You just have to recognize it.

How often do you mistake knowing something conceptually for actually experiencing it? If I ask you, *Do you know what an apple is?* perhaps an image of an apple comes to mind. It could be good, bad, organic—different apples for different people. You probably conclude that you know what an apple is. But is your idea of an apple the same as an apple? No. If it were, you could eat your idea. When you create an image of an apple and look at it, you say you know what an apple is. But you can touch a real apple; you perceive it directly. You can taste the apple, and it nourishes you. Direct perceptions connect us to the truth of being. Thoughts do not. Thinking you understand something is not enough. Feeling something, experiencing it directly, is much more powerful. That is embodied knowing. When you feel the space of being and connect with it, thoughts lose their power to define you or your experience, and they no longer dominate you.

When your thoughts carry you away, it is not a good sign. But if you are fully present in the spaciousness of being, thoughts and sensations become ornaments of that space, rather than distractions. A bird's song, for example, rather than disturbing your meditation, will highlight the peacefulness of it. A display of art is an ornament of space and light. But when an ornament carries you away and you no longer feel space and light, then you are lost.

Sometimes we are uneasy with openness. We feel too exposed. We are used to our familiar boundaries, and when they begin to dissolve it can be uncomfortable. Discomfort is a very human response. Can you allow a feeling of unease to rest in openness? Can you perceive the space directly and continue to rest your mind in it? Can you allow a feeling of loneliness to rest in the space? Or a feeling of disorientation? Space is the inner refuge. Trust that it is your friend, not your enemy. It will support you, so you will no longer feel lost. The spaciousness of being will allow you to feel complete and at peace rather than empty and unsettled. Trust space in the way a child rests in the arms of its loving mother. It is your home, not a strange place but the most sacred place. When you recognize that, your fear releases.

There are times when we feel lost or disoriented and don't know how to move forward in life. How can we find some direction when we are lost? When you experience a sense of being lost, ask yourself, *Who is the one who feels lost?* Bring open attention to this sense of self, the *I* who feels lost. Focus inward without moving from thought to thought or moving away from any feelings of discomfort. If you can embrace with openness the self who feels lost, that pain identity will start to dissipate and healing will begin. You realize that nobody is lost. And when the inner space of your being is no longer occupied with being lost, that space becomes available to you in more creative ways.

According to the teachings of dzogchen, you will never find your authentic self because your authentic self was never lost. This means that the mind that searches for what is missing needs to stop searching. The one who is feeling lost has to release its identity. In my tradition there is a saying: *In what is not there, you will find presence.* What does that mean? Let's say you have two pages open before you. One page represents open space. The other is the feeling of being lost. So here you are, focused on the experience of being lost. When you and this sense of being lost are intertwined, and you are looking through the eyes of the one who is lost, you are lost today, you were lost yesterday, and when tomorrow comes, yes, you will still be lost. You don't realize that you keep looking at this single page of the story of your life. Then one day you are guided to a different page—the inner refuge. Wow! The one who was feeling lost is gone. What has happened? The absence of the self who is saying *I'm lost* is all that happened. And in this absence you experience a dawning presence, the presence of being. You have a sense of coming home to yourself.

In discovering the space of being, you discover the base of creativity. Sometimes it is not immediate; it is not like turning a switch on or off. Through meditation you need to cultivate trust as well as deepen familiarity with the open space of being and the natural energy that arises from it. There is no right or wrong place to discover the power of openness. When you feel a sense of trust strongly enough, you can discover the space of being in every moment.

You can prepare for a creative moment by having your canvas primed and your paintbrushes ready, but maybe that morning, when you stand before the easel, nothing comes. Then in the afternoon, while you are standing on the platform at the train station, your mind is flooded with images. Creative inspiration can show up in odd places. As you become more familiar with the space within yourself, you can access creativity wherever you are.

Sacred expression is the ability to feel and connect with your true nature and express yourself from that place. According to the teachings, this is a great achievement. Anytime you are in the inner refuge, dynamic energy is present and expression naturally follows. If expression is not flowing, then you are disconnected—in the dark. Everything is different when you are connected.

Meditation:
Discovering the power of openness

To discover the power of openness, the source that is available in each moment, bring your attention to the crown chakra, a place in the body conducive to feeling a sense of spaciousness. This energetic center is where an upright human being touches the sky above.

Bring your attention to the crown of your head and rest your focus here. Let yourself settle. Feel the stillness of your body as a support for your focus. As you rest your attention at the crown, consider how you experience the vastness of the sky above you. Can you feel expansiveness, a release of boundaries, even the sense of wonder you might have felt as a child when you looked up at the sky? Imagine that the crown of your head is energetically open to the sky. As you continue to rest your attention here, aware of the space above you, feel the space within you opening up. Rest your focus here. Feel the stillness of your body as a support for tethering the moving mind, enabling you to discover the spaciousness within you, here and now.

As you rest, supported by stillness, your focus will naturally open, and you will become aware of the space within and around you. Thoughts, feelings, sensations, and memories may arise, but supported by stillness, you can just let them be. There is no need to follow them. But if you do, when you become aware that you have disconnected from the support of stillness, simply bring your attention back to the opening at the crown of your head and rest there. As you rest, you are supported by the unbounded spaciousness of being. You *are* that sacred space.

This is the first refuge: the unbounded spaciousness of being. Abide here as long as your experience is fresh and uncontrived.

Dedicate the merit of your practice with the aspiration: *In liberating my own being, may I benefit others.*

During this meditation, you might feel, *Oh, this would be a good time to think about my problem and come up with a creative solution!* I would discourage you from doing that, however. When you *think* about finding a solution, you are empowering your thoughts. Instead, simply be—and be aware of just being. You might wonder, *If I discourage my thoughts, what will be left of me?* The answer is, a lot! But the mind that asks that question is the thinking, moving mind, and that mind doesn't want to agree with the view that our truer intelligence is the awareness of being, of the source. Thinking does not want to lose its supremacy.

According to the dzogchen teachings, your essence is boundless. The first energetic location, at the crown chakra, supports you in discovering this sense of unbounded openness. This sacred dimension of being is referred to as the *dharmakaya*, the body of emptiness. It is always good to be as open as possible, though it is not always achievable. For me, turning toward the inner refuge helps. Then every day becomes an amazing experience. What I see, what I feel, and the decisions I make are the result of my connection to the inner refuge of being. I have no doubt about the truth of the openness of being. I can look back over the years and see times when I was confused and didn't know what to do. But when I turned in the right direction—toward the openness of being—the right decision came forth. My sincere wish is that you too will discover that the openness of your being is a refuge that is trustworthy and has transformative power. Discovering that refuge is the essential first step of a creative life.

OM ~ THE POWER OF AWARENESS

Just as necessary for creativity as openness is the awareness that discovers openness and connects us to unbounded space. Awareness illuminates the space of being, activating infinite possibilities. We discover that we are alive with unlimited potential. Often we *think* we are aware. Or we equate awareness with thinking, with the ability to name or label or describe our experience. But the awareness that connects us with this unbounded quality of openness is not thought in the conventional sense. It is described as naked awareness—naked of the conceptual mind. This awareness is direct knowing, free of bias or opinion or hope or fear. Rather than experiencing the space of being as empty, you experience it as rich or full. You feel complete just as you are in the moment. The energetic location in the body that supports the awareness that illuminates the space of being is the throat chakra, and the syllable that symbolizes this is *OM*.

As you discover the space of being, you discover your creative potential. The only way you will not discover your creative potential is if you are stuck in your habitual pain body. Your pain body sees only pain, attracts pain, talks pain talk, lives with pain, sleeps with pain. Through the eyes of your pain body you do not see creative potential. But when you take a break from that pain identity, you see something different from pain, weakness, and lack of confidence. This second energetic location—the throat chakra—supports a sense of completeness. In the teachings, this sacred dimension of being is the *sambhogakaya*, the body of light.

If you look within yourself at any given moment, it is possible to feel complete. But do you feel complete? Very often we don't. Deep inside we lack a connection to the spaciousness of being. We refer to spaciousness as a refuge, because discovering spaciousness heals the suffering of separation from our true nature. Awareness heals the pain of unworthiness. When we are not aware of the spaciousness of being, we feel that something is missing. We feel a lack of worthiness, and we are shy about approaching the outer world. We carry a sense of limitation: *I'm not good enough. I can't do this.*

What do you require in order to feel complete in any given moment? Can you list a few things? Everyone will have a different list, and the length of that list will vary. Some items on your list will be concrete: *I want to lose weight, clear the clutter from my house, be kinder to my mother.* Others will be more nuanced: *I want someone to love who will love me; I want to complete this body of work; I want to contribute something to society.* Everyone will have some response to this question.

Now let's say you are able to check off a few items on your list. Then if you are asked again, *Do you feel complete?* you will probably say, *Well, not really. I think I missed something. I need to update my list.* So you go back to list-making, but again you probably won't experience a feeling of completion even if you realize your goals. The sense of inherent completeness that the teachings point to does not require anything from the external world. You can be poor and feel a sense of completeness; alternatively, you can be rich and not feel complete.

We discover the sense of completion by drawing naked attention inward and connecting with openness. When I use the word *openness,* I'm referring to a very specific dimension within yourself—unbounded spaciousness. As we explored in *A,* we access unbounded spaciousness through stillness. In any given moment, as I become more conscious of that spaciousness within myself, I feel complete as I am in the moment. This sense of being complete is not about having something. It is the truth of your essential nature. You are the great completeness you have been searching for. But you cannot find it with the mind that searches for it. To discover unbounded spaciousness, you need to look directly inward without following the movements of your restless mind. Awareness, naked of thought, discovers unbounded spaciousness. This awareness is the second transformative power.

So the first discovery is connecting with the space itself. The second discovery is being *aware* of that connection. Naked awareness activates creative potential, and the result is an inner sense of resourcefulness. If you are only superficially aware of how you are sensing or feeling or thinking in any given moment, you will not discover the true resourcefulness I am talking about. People express this lack of connection in different ways, but it all comes down to a feeling that something is missing. What's missing is a deep sense of worth. When we feel something is missing, we often reach for something to fill the void. But this second creative potential is realized only when you feel connected to the space of being within you, not to something external. Connecting to the space within, you discover the infinite possibility of your essential nature.

Dzogchen is not only translated as "great perfection" but also as "great completeness." All positive qualities such as love, compassion, joy, and equanimity are already present in our natural mind. But often we don't know this. The challenge is to realize it. This realization conquers hope. What do I mean by that? The conventional meaning of hope (*I want X to happen*) is the opposite of fear (*I don't want X to happen*). Hope as an aspiration or prayer can be beautiful, but by imagining a particular outcome, you actually limit or block the unlimited potential of the natural mind. When you connect with the unbounded space of being, you can go beyond both hope and fear. The ultimate sense of freedom is realizing the infinite potential of your true self. That means releasing the limitations of your ideas. If you have a mind-set of what is perfect, that is an obstacle to other perfections. You've already set up your idea of perfection. To experience the inherent perfection of any moment, you must realize that in bringing your idea of perfection to the moment, you obscure the other possibilities that exist. The perfection you are trying to create or achieve probably will not happen, and you will not see the perfection that already exists within you. That is an even bigger loss.

Meditation:
Discovering the power of awareness

To realize naked awareness that discovers the source within, bring your attention inward to the throat center and rest your attention here. As you focus here, listen to inner silence. Silence does not mean there is an absence of sound, but rather that inner and outer sounds lose their power to capture or distract you. If you do become distracted, simply bring your focus back to the silence. If you have a persistent tendency to mentally comment on your experience, use a strong focus on silence as a support for releasing this habit. As this tendency begins to exhaust itself, you can relax your effort and rest, supported by the silence.

As you rest, the inner dialogue that defines you or defines an experience you are having begins to release its grip. When you stop struggling to change your experience or make sense of it, it releases, and you will feel a sense of peace. Awareness dawns that is fresh. You are present and aware of being present. You may experience the world with new eyes, open to the vividness of each moment. It is as if you are connecting with the dance of stillness and the melody of silence. You have a sense of being complete as you are in this moment. Abide here as long as your experience is fresh.

Dedicate the merit of your practice with the aspiration: *In liberating my own being, may I benefit others.*

Resting your focus in stillness at the crown with *A*, you open to the unbounded space of being. Now as you rest your focus at the throat center with *OM*, and you are aware of the space of being, you discover unlimited potential. This discovery brings a sense of richness, fullness, completeness. But just as fear can be an obstacle to openness, unworthiness can obscure the fullness of the moment. Everything you do reflects how you feel about yourself, how you value yourself. As you rest your attention on inner silence, the voices of criticism and judgment may be loud. But if you continue to listen to, hear, and feel the silence that is always available, those voices will lose their power. The silence that is empty of those voices is full of possibility.

As you have discovered, your ego identity needs to be maintained to exist. When you stop feeding the mechanism of ego with inner dialogue and feel the support of inner silence, the unworthy self falls away and the worthiness of the natural mind emerges. You feel like you are waking from a trance. You lose one self—the one with the unworthy self-identity—and discover another self that is inherently rich with possibility.

As the inner voices recede, awareness dawns that is fresh and free, naked of concepts. You are simply aware of being present in the moment. As you rest, let everything be as it is. Awareness illuminates the openness of being. This awareness is the second refuge and the second creative potential.

How might the awareness of openness affect your creative process? Sometimes when you try to express something—bring it into form—fear of failure comes up. But when you connect to the sacred space within you, which is full of infinite potential, you are connecting to your inner worth. This connection is a natural protection from thoughts like *I can't do it.* You accept yourself fully. You are who you are, complete and worthy. That awareness energizes you and stimulates the desire to express. Then, even if your expression is not met with approval, it won't throw you off or shut you down.

If you have found that source of creativity within yourself, you cannot lose. Whatever you want to do, you can do it. It is even possible that a result you *didn't* expect becomes the best thing you have ever done. People have sometimes found their greatest inventions in their mistakes, not in what they were going after. When you are open to discovering anything, not just what ego hopes to find, you experience a sense of infinite possibility that is not limited by hope for a specific outcome.

HUNG ~ THE POWER OF INSPIRATION

With *A* and *OM* we discover the joy of being. Now with *HUNG* we connect with the joy of being in the process of doing something. But we cannot truly find joy when we are living with unexamined pain. Being aware of a pain identity is necessary in order to discover that the ego is not as solid as it seems. As the ego dissolves, new possibilities emerge.

The third creative potential on the path to expressing yourself fully is the birth of positive qualities such as love, compassion, joy, and equanimity. Among these, joy is one of the most essential to creativity. Late one afternoon, when I was trying to finish an important project, instead of drinking coffee for an energy boost, I decided to reflect on all the truly wonderful people in my life. As I imagined the face of each person, I experienced their care, their love, their wish for positive things for me. I had not even finished reflecting on everyone who had come to mind before I was overwhelmed with joy. The beauty of those present in my life gave me all the energy I needed to finish the work I was doing.

If we look at what there is to appreciate in our lives, there is so much, but often we don't look in the right places. If you are not experiencing joy in the moment, something is holding you back. Though you may not be aware of it, you are stuck in your pain body, pain speech, or pain mind. If nothing reminds you to shift your view, pain eyes are the eyes through which you look at life. When there is no inner prompt encouraging you, reminding you, giving you a little push, you can get stuck in your pain, and when you look through pain eyes, you see only what is going wrong. The one who is looking is in pain and cannot see any bliss. You need to be aware of inner space and access joy, so you can see the world more positively. It is important to know that there's another way to look than through eyes of pain.

Let's say you are feeling the way I was the other afternoon: After a long workday, you are tired and just want to stop what you are doing. At that moment, you might even hear yourself muttering a familiar mantra: *I can't wait until this is over.* That internal voice becomes louder and louder, while physically you experience tension in your body. Chances are, you are tightening your abdomen, holding your breath, and endlessly repeating, *I can't wait until this is over.* You are now giving more energy to the pain of wanting the project to be over than to the project itself. Even worse, you don't even realize that you are draining your energy. But the moment you become conscious of what you are doing to yourself, you can stop. You can be still and be present with the pain in your body. You can draw your attention to inner silence and be with the pain speech you are generating. If you stay present with the experience you are actually having, it is possible to experience a shift. But if you simply accommodate the pain and think that it's normal to feel that discomfort, then you are in trouble. It is essential to realize you are suffering before you can stop.

So when you become aware that you are suffering, what should you do? The instruction is: *Don't do anything.* Simply draw your attention to the space within and around you. Just feel the space. That's *A*. The source of creativity is sacred space, which can be accessed in any given moment through stopping and feeling stillness, hearing silence, or being aware of spaciousness. The source is right here. You simply need to draw your attention to it in this moment. It takes a shift in attention and the right strength of attention to shift your energy and discover the source within. This is the first creative potential. Trust that you can do it.

But perhaps you shift your attention to stillness and not much happens. What then? You are aware of openness, but your connection to it is not strong enough. You need to remain present to the openness long enough to discover the second creative potential—*OM*—the connection to the source, the liveliness of the sacred space of being. As you feel this connection, you begin to feel confidence. No longer are you connected only to your pain through your resistance to what you're experiencing or expressing. When you draw your attention to stillness, it automatically loosens the connection to your resistance.

The openness of being becomes available, and in that openness a new sense of yourself emerges.

Whereas previously you were feeling blocked, agitated, resistant, now you are feeling connected and alive. You may not experience this shift right away or every time you practice. If you don't experience it, you may think you just have to try harder. That is the wrong approach. In order to discover the third creative potential— the power of inspiration—just be. If you allow space, allow awareness, joy emerges. Sometimes the experience of joy is intense; sometimes it is subtle. Either way, the seed of inspiration is there.

A seed must be in the right soil to germinate. If you plant a seed of inspiration in the soil of pain, it will not grow. That seed needs unbounded space and infinite awareness as its growing medium. You must hold your inspiration in open awareness. When you put a seed in the earth, it needs the warmth of the sun to sprout. Let's say a seed will sprout after 10 hours of the sun's warmth. While the sun is shining on the soil, the sun is not saying *I'm getting a little stressed out here waiting for something to happen. It's been eight hours already. I'm feeling some resistance to this whole germinating thing.* Do you think the sun would say that? Is the sun or the air or the water getting stressed out? Of course not. So if you hold an inspiration or intention in the space and warmth of being without impatience, and simply allow yourself to feel the warmth of open awareness, it will be just a matter of time before the seed sprouts. Patience is necessary. Every second of warmth contributes to the emergence of new growth. It's not about waiting for a particular result but marveling at the process. The process itself is sacred, joyful. In this process you are discovering the third creative potential: the power of inspiration.

As you are reading this, are you connected to the first creative potential? Do you feel the space of being, or are you sitting in your pain on your rotten karmic pain cushion? Do you see the infinite possibility in any given moment, or are you secretly focused on what is *not* happening in your life? Do you feel spontaneous joy, or are you thinking, *Nothing's happening*? You have a choice to shift your attention from what is not working to what is possible. You can open your focus to the sense of infinite possibility that exists within you. From there, qualities that can change your life will emerge. This isn't wishful thinking. It's a shift of perception that can occur right here, right now.

When you experience resistance, you need to address the one who is resisting, the one who always notices what is lacking in a situation or hopes for something else to happen. If you become aware of your resistance, instead of focusing on what you think you should be doing or the outcome you want, shift your attention inward. Find the pain identity, the sense of yourself that is creating the resistance.

Often when we realize we are procrastinating or distracting ourselves, we think: *What is wrong with me? This is really a great project; why can't I just do it?* Don't get caught up in those thoughts. Host your discomfort, your pain, your avoidance. Embrace your experience with arms of space, light, and warmth. Your pain will respond in a completely different way. When you are neither denying your pain nor indulging it, it will release on its own.

Meditation:
Discovering the power of inspiration

Find a position that supports you in being comfortable and awake. Rest your attention on the stillness of your body. Let your mind settle, supported by the focus on stillness. As you experience a basic sense of the openness of being, listen to the inner silence. As you hear it, rest your attention in the experience of silence. Let the sounds within and around you be like waves in the deep ocean of silence in which you rest.

Connect with the freshness of awareness. Simply be aware of being.

Bring this sense of openness and awareness to your heart center. Release any effort and rest here. Let your thoughts be as they are. Without following or suppressing them, abide in open awareness.

When you are aware that you have been caught up in a thought or image, open your focus and rest in the openness. Allow the spaciousness of your being to support you. Be aware of the spaciousness.

As you abide, you may feel a sense of well-being. You are warmly present, connected to the source of creativity within. Be aware of this goodness, this warmth. Allow the warmth of your presence to nourish you fully as you abide. Feel this warmth throughout your being. This warmth is the fire of creativity, of inspiration. Allow the energy of inspiration to ignite within you.

Abide here as long as your experience is fresh.

Dedicate the merit of your practice with the aspiration: *In liberating my own being, may I benefit others.*

This sense of well-being, this natural warmth, is the third inner refuge, the body of great bliss. The energetic location of the heart supports us in experiencing this sense of well-being and the warmth of positive qualities. In the Bön and Buddhist teachings, this sacred dimension of being is the *nirmanakaya*, the manifestation of enlightenment for the benefit of others.

Connected to the inner refuge, we can transform a pain body, pain speech, or pain mind into creative expression that benefits others. As you connect with your heart center, you can work with the obstacles that have

arisen in your life. To work with obstacles, I suggest offering your pain body, pain speech, or pain mind a spacious,
luminous, warm hug. We all understand what a hug is. As
humans, we need spiritual, social, emotional, and physical connections with one another to flourish. The metaphor of offering your experience a hug is directly related
to the teachings on inner refuge. A good hug needs to be
open and spacious, the first quality of the inner refuge.
But there are big differences in how you experience the
connection physically and energetically. We have all had
hugs that were open and inviting, whereas others may
have seemed perfunctory. Giving yourself a spacious hug
requires being open to your experience and, specifically,
to your pain.

In a good hug, connection is key. Awareness is connection. Luminous refers to awareness. To transform your
pain you must connect with it and with the openness of
your being. Naked awareness is that connection. So in relation to your pain, you need to be both open and aware.

The third aspect of a hug is the quality or warmth of
connection. It's not as if two rocks are coming together.
Some hugs have an abundance of warmth, others have
little; the degree of warmth is determined by the level
of luminosity and connection. The level of connection
depends on how open to each other the huggers are. The
quality of warmth comes from the depth of connection,
and the depth of connection depends on how open or
spacious you are. *Spacious*, *luminous*, and *warm* are inter-
related, connected, interdependent.

The self who needs to be embraced is obviously not
your true self, but the pain identity you currently feel
yourself to be. Embracing that pain self is a necessary part
of the process of transformation. The pain identity must
be acknowledged with open awareness, not met with

judgment or expectation. You need to meet the one in pain without trying to manipulate or change or punish that pain identity.

In Buddhism we talk about having compassion for all sentient beings. From the Buddhist point of view, suffering comes from ignorance of our true nature—from lack of self-realization. We suffer because we have not realized who we truly are, not because we are inherently sinful. This is not a punishing view but one of compassion.

If we look at ourselves through eyes of compassion, when we suffer, when we are lost, this lost sense of self who is suffering needs acceptance, care, and love, not expectations, judgment, or criticism. And yet if we listen to our internal voices, they are often very judgmental. This does not help toward transformation. Our suffering needs acknowledgment and compassion. In the dzogchen teachings, the way to acknowledge suffering is clearly defined. We do not feed the suffering ego by creating another, smarter ego that says, *Oh, I see you are suffering. I will give you compassion.* Instead, the spacious, luminous warmth of the natural mind meets suffering directly. This does not feed the mechanism of ego.

So first it is necessary to recognize that you are in pain—to see it and feel it without criticizing yourself. You need to host your pain and the one who is in pain. If you connect with stillness while you experience your pain and your pain identity, stillness will support you in connecting directly and intimately with your actual experience in the moment. Even more, stillness will support you in feeling spacious. A spacious hug is not grasping or self-grasping. It is not contracting or holding, but allowing, opening, clearing, liberating. You are not even holding on to an expectation: *Oh, I hope this pain will go away.* You are present and open in the moment, aware of what is and not trying to change or manipulate it, because the space you are aware of will allow your pain to release—to self-liberate. Your awareness illuminates the space. But if you judge or criticize yourself for being in pain, there is no warmth. It's not a warm hug—it's a mean hug, a cold hug.

It's strange that we expect acknowledgment and warmth from others but don't offer this to ourselves. We want others to be kind to us, but we are not kind to ourselves. We continue damaging ourselves through negative self-talk. So instead, be open without expecting anything. Be aware of your thoughts and feelings as they are without judging them, and allow yourself the warmth of kindness. As you are looking directly at your experience and your sense of yourself in the moment, the pain identity is becoming less fixed or solid because you are no longer feeding it with your thoughts or judgments. A new space opens up in you. And as you connect with this newly emerging space, your awareness of it evokes warmth and kindness. This kindness is not a product of effort but the natural result of openness and awareness. Sometimes it takes only 10 or 20 minutes of meditation to witness the dissolution of pain and feel the emergence of warmth.

But our pain, once acknowledged, is not our main focus. Now we need to become aware of the source, not the appearances. Many spiritual traditions instruct us to be mindful of appearances but lack the instruction to be aware of the source. When you are meditating, of course it is good to be aware of the thoughts, sensations, or emotions that are arising. If you are anxious, it is important to be aware that you are feeling anxiety. But the power of meditation comes not only from being aware of anxiety but also from connecting to the *source* of the anxiety. The source is not the event—the presence of anxiety. Rather, it is the space of being. The guidance is to be aware of that space, to be connected to it. As you connect to it, you are able to embrace the anxiety. You are aware of both the space and the anxiety. The anxiety is impermanent and changeable, but the space of being is unchanging. When you are connected to the unchanging source, whatever arises in that space eventually dissolves. The space of being is the ultimate healer.

Meditation:
Offering your pain identity a spacious, luminous, warm hug

Take a comfortable position. Become aware of your breath. Allow your breath to support you in releasing effort. Rest your attention on the stillness of your body. Through the stillness of your body, become aware of inner stillness, the stillness of being. Rest here. The stillness of being is a refuge, a sacred space.

Become aware of inner silence. As you breathe, let your exhalation support you to release any pain speech. Breathe it out. With each exhalation, rest more deeply in the inner silence. Listen to and hear the silence, feel the silence, be aware of the silence. Continue to use each exhalation to release any tendency to get caught up in inner dialogue. Rest, supported by inner silence. As the power of inner voices to distract you diminishes, awareness dawns free of thought. Awake and present, abide there.

Now bring your attention to the space in and around your heart. Breathe out the tendency to get caught up in thoughts, distractions, or doubts. Awareness of the breath can clear thoughts as the wind moves the clouds, giving access to the boundless space of the sky. Feel that inner sky, the sacred space within, as you clear thoughts with your breath.

Rest, aware of inner stillness, inner silence, and inner spaciousness. These three support you to rest deeply in the sacred space of being, in your true self.

Connected to this source within, gradually become conscious of something in your life that is disturbing you. You may be experiencing sickness or physical pain, an emotional challenge or difficulty with a loved one, or a challenge at work. Simply be aware of one place in your life where you experience pain. Be aware of how this pain lives in your body. Be aware of any tension and sensation. Be aware of inner dialogue—pain speech— and any emotions that may be present. Be aware of the movement of your mind—your thoughts and imagination. Let stillness, silence, and spaciousness support you in being present and allowing your experience fully. In this way you are hosting your pain.

Neither ignoring nor exaggerating your pain or your sense of yourself, connect with the presence of boundless space, pure awareness, and genuine warmth. Be aware that your experience of pain may shift or clear, but don't try to do anything with your experience other than be aware of the presence of openness, awareness, and warmth.

The power of being will heal the one who is in pain. The light of awareness will heal the darkness of pain. The warmth of your presence is a healing warmth. Rest here.

Like a loving mother responding to the needs of her child, see and feel your pain as if it were your child and bring full, loving, kind attention to your pain as you hold it with arms of spaciousness, awareness, and warmth. Awareness is the mother. Your pain is the child, immature and needing support. Feel the loving-kindness, care, and compassion that arise from the sacred space of being and allow healing to take place.

As pain decreases and blockages clear, more space opens up. Rest your attention here. From this clear space, you will experience a fresh sense of being. A sense of warmth or well-being will emerge. Allow the warmth. Feel yourself rich with kindness, care, warmth, and compassion. Kindness emerges from the sacred space of being as pure water springs from the earth. Let the waters of kindness quench your thirst.

Dedicate the benefit of your practice to all beings who are suffering or who are in the process of healing, with the aspiration that they may find their way to liberation. Hold this aspiration in your heart as you repeat: *In liberating my own being, may I benefit others.*

When the experience of being blocked or stuck or in pain begins to release, you may experience a sense of loss: *Who am I if I am not my struggle?* You are at a loss without the driving force of the effort to improve yourself. But can you let the sense of loss become your doorway to a new space? Inspiration, the sacred fire of creativity, does not come from struggle but from openness itself.

To discover something where you have lost something is the challenge. We feel more alive in the presence of ego. When ego is gone for a moment, we yawn and lose interest. But we can discover something here. It requires strength to remain present and attentive long enough to discover something in the space where you are experiencing loss or disorientation. But if you stay present and honor this space with your open attention, energy comes. According to the teachings, energy—creative vision—comes from the union of openness and awareness. But often we give up too early in the process. We lose heart. We shift our attention to something, anything else. Instead of shifting our attention, we need to recognize loss or disorientation as the place to rest our attention. When we do so, creative fire awakens. My teacher advised me many times: *In what you do not find, abide.* In other words, we have to trust that space and engage with awareness long enough for inspiration to awaken.

There is a traditional Tibetan teaching story in which a student is sent out to look for a yak. The student comes back at the specified time and says to the teacher, "I'm sorry. I did not find a yak." To which the teacher replies, "You found the *absence* of yak!" Most students would think they had failed the yak task. Few would realize that finding no yak was a noteworthy result and be able to say: "I searched for a yak and found something more interesting than a yak. I found the absence of yak!" Finding the space of being can happen when you search for the ego, the self, and your experience of not finding anything solid is strong enough to convince you that deep inside you are free. *In what you do not find, abide.*

In the process of discovering space and awareness—the absence of yak—you can begin to lose your intensity of focus. Why is this? Because your ego, your pain imagination, was the main way you experienced a sense of liveliness and now you are losing that. You might become disoriented or even bored because nothing appears to be happening. Traditionally, the obstacle in meditation at this point is called *lack of strength*. You experience a lack of presence in the absence of ego. But it is only when you lose the ego that you can find the authentic self. When you have focus and wakefulness and awareness in the absence of ego, you experience authentic presence. And in that presence you find playfulness and confidence, because the struggling forces of hope and fear no longer drive you. This is the way the sacred creative fire ignites. You are inspired by the freedom you taste and the desire to help others.

RAM ~ THE POWER OF RIPENING

The fourth stage on the path to realizing your creative potential is to recognize a sense of readiness. This means seeing the potential for expression in any given situation. Everything is possible. There is a story about two men who go to a new country to try and sell shoes. Most people in that country walk barefoot or wear simple sandals. So one man thinks, *I cannot possibly be successful selling shoes here because nobody in this country wears shoes.* But the other man thinks, *This is the best place to sell shoes because most people in this country are not yet wearing shoes! The market is wide open!*

Look at the difference between these two people. They go to the same place to sell the same product, and one sees infinite possibilities while the other sees only obstacles. I use this story to show that it is not *what* we are looking at but *who* is looking that determines the result. In any given moment we can reflect: *Whose eyes am I looking through?* When I am looking through eyes of lack or insecurity, I will see obstacles. When fear looks at the world, it discovers only enemies. When sadness looks at the world, it discovers loss. When the creative mind looks at the world, it sees possibilities. Seeing the possibilities in any given moment is the fourth creative potential.

You may be sitting in the midst of an unexpressed life. You might have warm feelings for others that you don't express, ideas and visions that are unfulfilled, projects that are incomplete. Often as an exercise I will make a list of what in my life is almost ready to happen but only needs a little energy or attention from me to reach completion. Become aware of the things around you that are ready to be expressed but aren't quite happening because you have not appreciated this state of readiness. When you are fully aware of what is in this state of readiness, you don't have to do much. You just have to say *Yes!* and do it.

Perhaps you live with someone you care about deeply. But when was the last time you expressed the warmth of connection that you feel? The connection is alive, and love is there, but you simply haven't expressed it. When I teach meditation, I often emphasize this aspect of expressing the results of the practice. I suggest that my students draw attention to the right places—for example, to their loved ones. After just a few sessions of meditation, people are crying because they realize they have feelings they haven't expressed. It's amazing to watch their bodies soften and their field of energy change when they realize that they haven't paid attention to the connection with those they love. Why is it we neglect this?

Many times we are so busy focusing on the people we have problems with that we overlook the ones we really love. But if we spend our time on problematic people, we have no time left to nurture the love that is already here. We are focusing in the wrong place. What sometimes happens then is that we start to lose the good feelings for the people we love.

Relationships need care and attention. They need the water of our kindness, the fire of our humor and joy, the air of our curiosity and inquiry, the earth of our warmth of connection. If a houseplant is not watered, it will die. In any given moment of your life, there is creative potential that is dying through lack of attention. So not only are you not accomplishing what you want, but you are losing what you have. This is very sad.

The fourth creative potential discovers the possibilities where you have inspiration but haven't fulfilled it. If you reflect on your life, you can see ideas and inspirations and endeavors and relationships that were alive once but are languishing now. They had incredible potential, but as a result of your not giving them sufficient attention, they are unfulfilled. Be conscious of what is present in your life now. Don't dwell on what is gone. It's more important to see what needs your attention now, so you can rededicate yourself and not lose your inspiration and vision.

Why are we so attracted to what is not working in our lives? When something is not working, we tend to dwell on it. We think about it and talk about it and then try not to think about it and talk about it. But either way, we are not addressing the subject—the one who is thinking and talking. Instead, we are addressing the object—our thoughts. The focus shouldn't be on what is not working, because even if we change the focus, our misery will find a way to express itself. It may find a better, nicer, subtler, more complex, more personal, or more sophisticated way, but it is all the same thing: pain imagination.

As we have seen, it's always a question of who, not what, because the one who is thinking is in pain, and pain loves to think about pain. Pain needs to talk about pain. Pain seeks others with pain. Pain seeks what is familiar—pain. Pain is afraid of unfamiliar situations like openness and unbounded space. If you are able to acknowledge your fear of openness, you can turn to the supports we have been exploring that are always available—stillness, silence, spaciousness—and embrace the self who is afraid. You can show up for the one in pain and offer a spacious, luminous, warm hug. As your pain identity feels the warmth of your open attention, it dissolves. When you address *who* properly, your pain imagination stops. Space opens up within you and within your life. You discover the fourth creative potential—the drive and fire within. Your pain releases its power to hold captive your positive qualities.

How can you champion and cultivate your creative fire? By bringing your open and warm attention to it. Invest your attention in the right places. Reflect on what brings you alive. Talk about what you love in your life. Reflect on what you love in your family members. It is so easy to focus and talk about what we don't like. That is often the default pathway. I have heard many detailed life stories from my students, and with some of my students, I don't even know how many family members they have, because I only hear about one person—the sister or mother who never seems to love and accept them.

I want to hear about all the people you love. Who do you encounter at your work? You tell me who you have difficulty with, but I want to hear who you have a nice relationship with, who you work well with, who you enjoy collaborating with. Let's talk about what is alive in your relationships. Let's talk about what is alive through your senses. Let's talk about what moves you and inspires you in your life. If you don't reflect on what brings you alive, you could lose the connection to it. Every time you remember what brings you alive, it activates something in you—changes occur in your brain, in your body, in your breath. Recognizing what brings you alive brings positive energy and joy. We all experience sparks of inspiration and connection, but often we don't acknowledge them or reflect on them because we are too busy.

When the joy of inspiration and connection comes, notice the qualities that are present. You may feel a sense of freedom, curiosity, freshness, vividness. You may feel energized and inspired. When this happens, action becomes effortless and joyful. Instead of draining you, your actions give you strength.

So often we do something because we think we are supposed to. Then life becomes a chore. We feel heavy, tired. There is no space, no light; we feel no enthusiasm or warmth. We somehow believe we need to be in control in order for life to go well. Ego is always trying to take charge. But if you follow the path of inspiration rather than your agenda, you might discover that something else is available. But first, you have to go into that space of being that is truly unbounded and trust it. The more I invest my attention in the space of being, what emerges from it is of a very different quality than my agenda would suggest. When you go into that space, ego is not being fed. All forms of ego—thoughts, feelings, ideas—release their grip. There is naturally more space, and when you nourish the space with your awareness, a new sense of yourself arises, with fresh thoughts and fresh emotions.

If you have a new idea you want to express, just do it. What is holding you back? There are many reasons we hold back. We may think: *It might not work. I might mess it up.* Don't follow those voices. Just do it! Start right away. Don't be afraid of failure. If something works, great! If not, that's fine, too. It's much more fun to live life joyfully than to always be afraid that something might not work. Things don't always have to turn out the way you planned. If you look through eyes of openness and freshness, you will see goodness in whatever you do. You just haven't allowed yourself to see it before. Ego has prevented it. Ego has a diminished view of things. Consider self-respect, self-value, for example. Someone may pay you a compliment for something you have done, but often you meet it with, *Well, I was lucky there.* Or, *I'm surprised that turned out as well as it did.* It is as if we feel we have to qualify our successes or protect ourselves from the simple enjoyment of our accomplishments. We feel too naked or exposed. We need to embrace our fear of being seen, being acknowledged, and not listen to ego's pain speech.

The causes and conditions for new thoughts to emerge are space and awareness. Since they already exist within you, you don't even have to exert much effort to access them. Just say *Yes!* to the fresh idea that arises. When you feel energy and inspiration, fearlessly take action. Even if it is a familiar idea that didn't quite work before but you would like to try it again, take action. It might not work this time either, but guess what—it doesn't have to work. By giving your idea the space to *not* work, there is a greater chance that it *will* work, that a solution will be found. So, take action! Trust your inner intelligence. It is unscripted, improvisational. Dance with it. Recognize the distinction between what intuitively and spontaneously arises and what ego manipulates. When you recognize the difference, you will wholeheartedly say *Yes!*

When those moments happen in my life, I don't want to be the obstacle to what life is offering me. I say *Let's do it!* How much effort does it take to say yes to a good friend's invitation to Saturday night dinner? Many things in life are no more difficult than that, because the right causes and conditions are already present. But even when we think a project is valuable, it may not manifest because the right causes and conditions are not present. There have been times when I had difficulty implementing an idea, so it didn't work. Why feel bad? Not everything works. Giving energy to something that is not working or not giving energy to what is working is fruitless. If you put energy into what is working, so much can flow.

When you recognize that the causes and conditions are supporting your vision, at that point it is your commitment that counts. Don't hold back. Look at some of the decisions you have made that changed the course of your life. Can you see where you were open, where you said *yes* and something happened as a result? Follow the trail of *yes*. Don't dwell on what didn't happen, or what could have happened but didn't. Remember the times you followed your inspiration and bring your attention there. When inspiration arises, even if it is only a flash, your open attention will nurture it. A flash can spark a revolution. Take the leap and say *Yes!*

When a spark of an idea or inspiration is alive in you, it comes from the space of being, with awareness that is curious and free. But if you let your pain imagination interfere, your creativity will be blocked. You may still act, but your action will not be spontaneous; it will be tied to an outcome. Don't think of an outcome. Doing what you love with space and warmth is valuable and healing in itself. What matters is the liveliness that you feel. Sometimes we produce something good at the cost of much pain. That is a shame, because what matters is the process, not the outcome. You may have times when you are happy and feeling good, and what you express from that place is enjoyable. It could be a meal that you cook and share with another, or a walk you take where you noticed the play of wind through the grass. But you may discount such experiences. You shouldn't. It's essential to protect the integrity of your process from your thoughts about the outcome. The process itself needs to be valued. I'm not saying that you shouldn't have a goal, but the goal should not be your primary objective.

Your planning, goal-oriented mind should not be in charge of your life. How long have you been planning to be happy? If you look at why you are not happy at the moment, you might say, "Well, I'm in the middle of a project right now." Can't you be happy in the middle of your project? If you can't, you are looking at it in the wrong way, thinking, *When I finish this, I'll be happy*, or *When I get there*, or *When I see my friend*, or *On the weekend, I'll have some time to be happy*. If you are in the right space with the right awareness and the right perspective, you can be happy anywhere at any time. Even in situations in which you think you are supposed to suffer, you might actually feel good.

We need to recognize obstacles to creative flow and clear them, not feed them with our attention. Our attention needs to be free to connect with the freshness of the moment, to connect with openness. When you are in creative flow, an intuitive sense of how to move or speak spontaneously emerges. Space and light and warmth and enthusiasm are present. Trust that. Don't obscure the moment with your doubts and fears. Moments of doubt are always challenging. How many times have you had the experience of being so agitated that you could not even see the goodness in goodness? Think of a situation you find challenging. Recognize that it is your mind that is in conflict, not the situation. If you shift your attention inward and rely on the supports of stillness, silence, and spaciousness, you will connect with inner space and light and emerge with a different view. What you thought was unworkable no longer seems so. You see possibilities. When you are open, you see much more. You can look at a painful situation through eyes of wisdom and kindness and see the light and warmth within pain.

Sometimes while we are working on a project we have to make a decision about some detail, and suddenly we think that the whole project is worthless, that nothing we are doing really matters. At that moment, we may cast about for someone to affirm us. But instead, you can turn your attention inward. Find openness through stillness or silence or spaciousness, and when you have connected with yourself, embrace the pain you are feeling. Give this pain space and the light of awareness and the warmth of presence. If you allow your pain to breathe, it will naturally exhaust and release. But you need to remain connected to yourself throughout this process and feel the support of the inner refuge. As your doubt releases its grip, fresh ideas can emerge with fire and enthusiasm. The quality of these thoughts will be different from the quality of the thoughts you had only moments before. Once you notice this, you can move on those thoughts. You can act from a clear and open place.

Sometimes we lose the connection to our enthusiasm. If you are making bread, in order for the yeast to be activated so the dough will rise, you need to maintain heat. Similarly, in order for your creative inspiration to ripen into expression, you need to maintain the heat of awareness. Lose the heat and the process will stop. Apart from not losing the warmth of connection, there is nothing you have to do. Through effort we often force something to ripen when it is not ready. And then we are disappointed in the result or in ourselves. Instead, we just have to maintain awareness and connection. We lose awareness and connection because we are distracted. We need to be more focused and consistent. If when you wake up you see that the sun is shining, you might feel simple joy in the beauty of the day. You might feel a sense of freshness and warmth and feel great. But often this good feeling lasts only until you begin thinking of all you have to do. And throughout the rest of the day it doesn't even occur to you to connect with the sky and the light and the openness you felt earlier. Joy is fleeting. The day may still be beautiful, yet your awareness of its beauty lasted only moments. So, the key to joy is to remember to be aware of the sky and the light you appreciated as you woke up. Maintaining connection to any positive quality is a process of reconnecting again and again to the source of openness and freshness within that is always available to us.

Meditation:
Discovering the power of ripening

Assume a comfortable posture with your spine straight and your chest open. Place your hands in your lap in the position of equanimity. Bring your full attention to the stillness of your hands and rest your attention here. As you settle into stillness, release any imprint of effort with each exhalation. Connect with the stillness throughout your body. Gradually discover the stillness of being and rest here.

Listen to, hear, and feel the silence within and around you. Allow silence to support you to just be. Release the impulse to talk to yourself, to describe your experience. Rest supported by silence.

Bring your attention to the space within and around your heart, as if you were discovering the openness of the sky itself. Rest your attention in the openness, allowing all thoughts, feelings, sensations, and images to be as they are, without following or suppressing them.

Continue to allow each exhalation to support you in releasing any effort of body, speech, or mind. Trust the refuge of your being—the unbounded spaciousness, the liveliness of awareness, the warmth of presence.

As you rest, connected to the heart center, become aware of a sense of well-being, the warmth of presence. Begin to reflect on what moves you in life, what brings you alive through your senses. Notice what touches your heart in your relationships with others. Where are the sparks of love or joy in your life? Allow time to notice what inspires you.

Shift your attention to the navel chakra. As you rest your attention here, continue to invest your full attention in what is alive in you. The warmth of your open awareness ripens your inspiration. Feel a sense of *Yes!*—a commitment to nurture what inspires you. Continue to hold the space for positive energy, ideas, and visions that may emerge.

Rest your attention at the navel chakra as long as your experience is fresh.

Dedicate the merit of your practice with the aspiration: *In liberating my own being, may I benefit others.*

Working with emotional energy

Our emotional energy can derail us or be dynamic fuel for creative expression. Through meditation we can explore our emotions and give a spacious, luminous, warm hug to our emotional conflicts and unfinished business. Do you know what I mean by *unfinished business*? I am referring to life experiences that remain undigested. We have turned away from them or left them behind because they were uncomfortable, or we were too young or too frightened or not sufficiently supported to integrate them. But our undigested experiences do not leave us. They appear in our dreams; they appear in situations we encounter; they appear as people who enter our lives. Again and again we are brought to familiar painful places. The good news is that we can properly compost our experiences, allowing them to become the rich soil of our continued growth and expression.

Again, the advice in meditation in relation to any emotional experience is: *Leave it as it is.* My teacher repeated this phrase often. I needed to hear it again and again to integrate it fully into my life. How can we understand this pith instruction, this essential teaching? Let's take the metaphor of a pond. If the water in a pond is stirred up by the wind, it appears cloudy. The windier it is, the dirtier the pond appears. But if the air is calm, gradually the dirt and debris sink to the bottom of the pond, and the water becomes clear. By not stirring the pond, by leaving it as it is, the water clears. For most of us, however, it is difficult to *leave it as it is*. When we have strong feelings, we feel that we have to *do* something, have to take care of something. It is hard for us to *leave it as it is*.

I encourage you to explore and trust these ancient teachings. Follow them with an open heart and apply them whenever you need them. Then you will experience what I am talking about. Your mind will be crystal clear. That's the nature of mind—it is always clear. The mind is like a lotus flower. Even though the lotus has its roots in the mud, its blossom is spotless. As with the lotus, so with the mind. No matter how much confusion and pain is present, this spotless, clear mind can be discovered right in the middle of the confusion and conflict. But often, we are not interested in discovering this mind. We are more interested in talking about that person who is causing us so many problems. When we are mired in internal pain and confusion and emotional drama, we are not looking at the space or awareness that is ever present.

Our hesitation to express ourselves fully and creatively in life comes from our conflicted emotions or mental pain. Basically, negative emotions are present because we don't know our true selves. That is the definition of ignorance. From this basic sense of disconnection from our true nature, negative emotions arise and we suffer.

The self-liberating nature of emotions

The idea of leaving it as it is, leaving what is in its own place, is a beautiful concept, a beautiful practice. If we leave an emotion as it is, it will liberate itself without any effort on our part, and we will be transformed as a result. For example, if I'm sad and I'm fully aware of it and I'm leaving it as it is, the sadness cannot sustain itself. But what usually happens is that our sadness triggers a story and the story drives our imagination. We anticipate our future interactions with others, which influences how we act, and the result is more confusion and pain. In this way, sadness and anger and any number of negative emotions are sustained. Sometimes you may even secretly like your emotional pain; maybe you've made friends through your shared sadness or righteous anger. But you are not leaving it as it is. You are attached to your sadness or anger. You are paying too much attention to it, or, more accurately, you are paying the wrong kind of attention to the emotion. That binds you to the emotion and blocks the expression of other possibilities.

There are many kinds of emotional pain. Sometimes our painful experiences seem to arise very randomly. *I made a fool of myself. Why do I always say the wrong thing? I don't belong here.* These seem to be branches of more deeply rooted dissatisfaction. Maybe you've been feeling taken advantage of or rejected by a friend, family member, or colleague. Perhaps this sense of yourself is familiar. These feelings may have been part of your life for many years. Perhaps you recognize a deep and familiar pain. You can laugh sometimes, but you still feel the pain. You can go to a party, you can do your work, and still you carry this pain with you. The pain is deeply present. And anytime you have an opportunity for conversation with someone you trust, this pain comes up. You could converse for hours on this topic, because it feels so firmly rooted. If you feel that you are really stuck with deep emotional wounds or pain, it's very important to acknowledge the pain properly. Merely discussing a problem is not acknowledging it properly. You may be complaining, getting angry, imagining revenge, but you are not truly acknowledging your pain. You need to get closer to your pain, feel your hurt, and then give it a spacious, luminous, warm hug. You may not have done that because you have not experienced enough support within yourself, so you keep circling around the pain through talking, complaining, criticizing, and judging. Many times you are the target of your own judgment, adding pain to pain.

What are the undigested emotional experiences that you carry? Your story is different from my story. His story is different from her story. Every story matters because there is a teller of that story who matters. The teller of your story is in pain. The teller of your story is seeking help. The teller of your story needs compassion and kindness. Your story matters.

The practice of reflection is a first step to healing emotional pain. No matter what situation has evoked the pain, you need to ask, *Is this pain familiar?* Then you can determine whether the pain is just situational or something that you have carried for a while. And then you need to ask, *Who is the one who is suffering?* so you can fully experience the pain identity that you see yourself to be. You can use this same inquiry to work with other pains and stuck places. You might find painful experiences anywhere in your relationships with yourself, your family, and the larger community. Each of us has many different experiences of self, all of which need our respect and care, and all of which are not who we truly are. Again and again, these identities block our creativity and the expression of our positive qualities. These deep, emotionally rooted pain identities continue to block us because they have not been properly acknowledged or met in the way they live in our body, emotions, and mind. It may be true that someone has treated you unfairly, but the healing of a pain identity happens only within you, by you. You need to make a commitment to show up for yourself—to bring spacious, nonjudgmental, warm attention to your pain. In showing up for yourself again and again, you will gain confidence that the inner refuge is always available to support you.

Taking the three precious pills
for emotional pain

There is so much to discover from the pith instruction *Leave it as it is*. But it is not always easy to do. Anytime you are having difficulty with this instruction, you can rely on the three precious pills. They will support you in developing the ability to leave it as it is. The moment you become aware of emotional pain, whether you are by yourself, engaged with someone else, or dealing with a professional challenge, taking one of the three precious pills will protect you, calm you, connect you, and help you find a sense of clarity and peace. After you take a precious pill, your reactivity will gradually ease and your pain may even disappear. You will feel a sense of inner freedom. Then what will you be aware of? Space. In that space, you experience freshness. New qualities spontaneously emerge. You are able to feel gentleness, kindness, and love, and you are able to give a spacious, luminous, warm hug to your pain identity. The healing medicine of self-compassion becomes available.

We have all had the experience of being carried away by emotion. When our emotions are making our choices, we feel victimized by our pain. Meditation practice both on and off the cushion supports us in staying present with our emotions. We begin to recognize the inner spaciousness that is always present, even when emotions are triggered. As we trust this spaciousness of being we find we *do* have choices.

When you recognize that you are being carried away by emotion, remember that you have a practice you can do right at that moment. Taking a precious pill is an action that can support you in being present to what you are feeling and protect you from reacting. You will be able to respond from a more openhearted place. Your response may surprise you because it comes spontaneously and genuinely. It is wonderful to be surprised in this way. When you feel the qualities of warmth, kindness, and compassion that emerge, you will be able to give a spacious, luminous, warm hug to your deeply rooted emotions. This may be the first time your emotional pain has received some acknowledgment and love. You may feel the experience so strongly that you are moved to tears.

DZA ~ THE POWER OF MANIFESTING

The fifth stage on the path to realizing your creative potential is the movement or flow from ripening to action. Bring to mind someone you love. Connect with the love and imagine a simple action you can take to express all you feel for this person. Can you see the relationship between direct attention to the quality that is present—in this case, love—and the expression of that quality? When you experience the presence of a quality such as love, how often do you express it? Most of us don't very often. As a result, our creative potential is not completely fulfilled.

I encourage you to recognize when a quality such as appreciation or gratitude is present in you and to give that quality a voice, a gesture, an expression. Whereas *RAM* matures the fire or the creative vision that is awakened in the heart, *DZA* supports us in taking action and expressing. So taking action is your fifth practice. But if you are struggling to express yourself, whether to a person, on a canvas, or in a poem, it is not yet time to take action. If you try to express when there is no fire, you are acting from effort, not inspiration, and your actions are not spontaneous.

So what do you do if you are struggling and recognize that you are disconnected from inspiration? Go back to the beginning of the map, to *A*. Discover the space within you in relation to the person, the canvas, the poem. If you don't have the space, you won't have *OM*, the connection. If you don't have the connection, you won't have *HUNG*, the necessary inspiration. If you don't have the necessary inspiration, you won't have *RAM*, the necessary fire or drive. If that is the case, where is *DZA*, action, going to come from? It will only be coming from your painful effort.

When spontaneous action is not available, don't push. Go to the space within, the inner refuge. The inner refuge is the single medicine for all varieties of suffering. Any problem, same medicine. Developing trust in that medicine is essential. When you connect with the inner refuge and rest in open awareness at each chakra center, the creative potential of that center is activated.

Meditation:
Discovering the power of manifesting

Assume a comfortable posture with your spine upright and your chest open. Place your hands in your lap in the position of equanimity. Bring your full attention to the stillness of your hands and rest your attention here. Gradually connect with the stillness throughout your body, releasing the imprint of effort with each exhalation.

Bring your attention to the crown chakra. As you rest your attention here and continue to settle into stillness, you will gradually discover the stillness of being. There is a gift here—the unbounded spaciousness of being, the source of creativity. Receive it as you rest in openness at the crown.

Shift your attention to the throat chakra. Listen to, hear, and feel the silence within and around you. Allow silence to support you to just be. Release the impulse to talk to yourself, to describe your experience. Rest supported by silence. Feel a sense of peace. As you rest, be aware of being. Awareness, free of bias, connects you to the openness of the source within and discovers possibilities. Connect with the gift of awareness of possibilities.

Now bring your attention to the space within and around your heart, as if you were discovering the openness of the sky itself. Rest your attention in the openness, allowing all thoughts, feelings, sensations, and images to be as they are without following or suppressing them.

Continue to allow each exhalation to support you in releasing any effort of body, speech, or mind. Trust the refuge of your being: unbounded spaciousness, the liveliness of awareness, and the warmth of presence at the heart.

As you rest, connected to the gift of warmth at the heart center, reflect on what moves you in life, what brings you alive through your senses, what touches you in your relationships with others. Where are the sparks of love or joy in your life? Allow time to notice what inspires you.

Shift your attention to the navel chakra. As you rest your attention here, continue to invest your full attention in what is alive in you. The warmth of your open awareness ripens your inspiration. Feel a sense of *Yes!*, a commitment to nurture what inspires you. Be open to positive energy, ideas, or visions that may emerge.

Now bring your attention to the secret chakra. As you rest your attention here, all the creative powers of openness, awareness, inspiration, and ripening flow into this center. Continue to release any effort as you allow the flow of connection here. Feel your readiness to express your life fully. Allow the flow of thoughts, images, or visions that support expression. Appreciate the gift of your life.

Rest here as long as your experience is fresh.

Dedicate the merit of your practice with the aspiration: *In liberating my own being, may I benefit others.*

We have explored how our habitual patterns of reactivity—our pain identities—block us from accessing the free and open space of our natural mind and the positive qualities that are available to us at any given moment. We can prepare the causes and conditions for manifesting our positive qualities, but the fruit, the benefit of our practice, arises spontaneously. Now, with *DZA*, we are no longer healing our pain identities and developing our talents. We are actively expressing our gifts and living to the fullest.

Meditation is not a passive practice but one that engages our attention and creative energy. As we have seen, it has the power to bring about profound positive change. Our commitment now is to action. To facilitate the process of integrating the benefits of meditation into everyday life, I have developed a four-step practice that my students and I have found effective in transforming obstacles to creative expression. I recommend that you record the process in a journal so you will begin to recognize positive changes that occur but might otherwise be overlooked or dismissed.

A Four-Step Transformation Practice

1. Reflect

Identify an opportunity for transformation: a situation, relationship, or experience in which you become reactive and a pain identity is active. Perhaps you feel bored or disconnected. Perhaps you feel stuck in a painful situation and keep replaying it in your mind. Perhaps you are talking repeatedly to yourself and others about it. Perhaps you feel heavy or agitated in your body. Pause. Turn your attention inward. Take a moment to be with your experience as it shows up in your body, speech, and mind. Notice what is drawing your attention most strongly as you sit with it. Notice any sensations in your body. Become aware of how your breath may be affected. Is there inner dialogue? Is there a story you are telling yourself? Reflect on any limited sense of yourself that you experience. Is this sense of yourself familiar to you? Is this a pattern that recurs in your life? Recognizing your reactivity becomes an opportunity for transformation as you bring it to your meditation practice.

2. Identify what supports you

Once you recognize your reactivity, identify what supports you in simply being with your experience. If your body is agitated, stillness may be the support you need, so rest your attention on the stillness of your body. If your breath is disturbed or you are talking to yourself, inner silence may be the support you need. Rest your attention on the inner silence—listening to it, hearing it, and feeling it. If your imagination is active with stories or scenarios, remember the support of spaciousness of mind. Open your attention to the support of the sky of the mind. Openness supports you in letting the thoughts and movements of your mind be as they are. As you are able to simply let them be, they will naturally let go. When you are feeling reactive, another support is to rest your attention at each chakra center and host your pain identity with openness, awareness, and warmth.

3. Describe the progression of the practice

It is important to begin your meditation practice without an agenda. Take time to release any effort in your body, speech, and mind, and simply feel the support of stillness, silence, and spaciousness. Then, as you connect to the inner refuge and experience a sense of well-being, bring to mind a challenge or pain identity and host it in your practice. As you host the challenge in your practice over time, notice any shifts that occur. When the challenge appears in your daily life, it is an opportunity for informal practice, for taking one of the precious pills. Journaling about your meditation experience, both formal and informal, will help you honor your path. It reinforces your intention and your ability to find the creative potential in any moment, particularly when you are struggling.

4. Result

As you live your life, notice any shifts in your experience. Is there any freedom or openness where previously you would have been reactive or judgmental? Do you notice an increased sense of well-being or the presence of any positive quality? Do you find yourself able to express or manifest in a way that you previously were not able to? It is important never to force a result. Instead, notice when changes spontaneously occur. Let yourself be pleasantly surprised by the sense of spaciousness or confidence that you begin to experience or the positive qualities that emerge. Noting these shifts in your journal will continue to illuminate the path of discovery.

It is important to appreciate the positive changes you experience as you continue to practice with the challenges in your life. A transformation is any positive change or shift in behavior experienced as a result of reflecting on a challenge or difficulty and applying the practices of formal and informal meditation. Habitual reactions and pain identities may show up in relation to yourself, your family and ancestors, your profession, or the wider world. In order to change your relation to the conditions you experience, you must have a taste of the indestructible quality of the space of being. That ultimate realization of the inner refuge is essential. This will support you in acknowledging the sense of self you are experiencing. As you host your experience it becomes a doorway to the creative source of being. Connected to this source within, you can express your life spontaneously and creatively.

DING—Confidence

Chapter 4

The Sacred Expression of Suffering and Wisdom

To live fully, we need to express our feelings, both positive and negative. If we don't, life becomes circumscribed. It becomes harder to engage with other people; it may even become hard to breathe.

But sometimes when we host a difficulty in the openness of being, it doesn't fully release, and we don't have access to our positive qualities. We're stuck. This doesn't mean that there is a lack of healing power in sacred space. It means that we got lost on the way to the inner refuge and didn't receive the medicine of the inner healer, the source within. Our connection to openness is not steady enough.

When we are blocked in this way, we may fear expressing our blocks, as often they are bound up in feelings of shame or guilt: *I'm not supposed to get angry. I don't want to hurt anyone. I should be a better person.* But all is not lost. It is possible to learn how to express negative or conflicted emotions without hurting yourself or anyone else in the process. The challenge is to express what you are feeling in the right way. The issue is not the form your expression takes but the space from which you express. Once you make a connection with stillness, silence, and spaciousness, when you feel blocked emotionally, you can safely release your feelings through movement, voice, writing, or some other means of expression.

There is a traditional Bön practice called *rushen*, in which the practitioner goes to a remote place to safely release blocked feelings. There, the practitioner might pretend to be a tiger or a mouse, imitating their sounds and movements to allow the repressed feelings to emerge. Resonating with the energetic vibrations of the animal releases energies that were blocked. But you don't have to roar like a tiger or cower like a mouse to release emotional blocks. Dancing, painting, writing, sculpting, cooking, singing, or gardening—anything that moves your energy—can be a powerful form of release. You can use whatever skills or inclinations you have as your vehicle for expressing emotion. In this way, you can acknowledge and honor your sadness or loneliness, and give your frustration or sense of injustice a voice.

When you release emotions, particularly negative ones, it is essential to recognize the space that opens up as the feelings release. From this space, positive qualities will emerge. And expressing strong feeling is not just a release for you; it can even be a gift to others. It is deeply moving to witness an expression of genuine emotion, whether it is sadness or joy.

I created two practices, rushen art and tögel art, that are based on the traditional Tibetan methods for clearing emotional blocks and connecting with the pure and open state of being. In rushen art, we express repressed emotions or other blockages from the inner refuge, the place of stillness, silence, and spaciousness. The inner refuge is the safe space that supports us in connecting with inner confusion or chaos and then releasing it through some form of expression. As we release the blockages, a fresh space opens up. Tögel art then allows us to express the positive qualities that spontaneously arise from the fresh space that opened up through rushen art.

Rushen comes from the Tibetan phrase kor de rushen. Kor means samsara, the grasping mind or ego, the impure self; de means nirvana, the enlightened state, the pure self; rushen means separating, distinguishing, clarifying. Kor de rushen refers specifically to separating samsara, the impure self, from nirvana, the open state of being that is our natural mind. Rushen practice involves exercises to clear the impure self and connect with the pure self. The practice of tögel, which literally means leaping over or crossing, involves expressing the spontaneity and liveliness of the pure self.

For most of us samsara and nirvana are not separate, not clearly distinguished from each other but intertwined. We are all fundamentally enlightened at the core, but at the same time the ego, the grasping mind, is ever present. Whenever the ego is involved, the mind becomes closed, agitated, or dull, preventing us from seeing our inner sacred qualities. When we are open, we have more access to our sacred being. Rushen art clears the impure self and gives us a glimpse of the pure self. Tögel art then allows us to fully express our true nature.

Rushen art and tögel art are considered sacred arts because they bring us closer to our essential nature. With these practices, we are working very deep within, uncovering what is untouched or denied. In rushen art, we allow ourselves to open to whatever is hidden and connect with feelings that have been suppressed, unexpressed, unconscious, limited, or blocked. Supported by the inner refuge, we permit ourselves to see these emotions clearly and express them skillfully. When the blockages are released, the positive qualities beneath them are revealed. Expressing those positive qualities is the practice of tögel art.

With rushen art, even dark and negative emotions are given a voice. You learn how to express any turbulence with awareness and warmth and kindness toward yourself. Suppressing emotions and holding on to blockages is like putting yourself in a dark room with no space or air; you feel as if you are suffocating. Releasing these feelings is emotionally liberating and healing.

Rushen art practice

There is no prescribed or ideal medium for expressing suppressed emotion through rushen art. You can choose whatever form attracts you. The first step in rushen practice is to connect with the blocked emotions that need to be expressed. Begin this process with reflection. What is important to you at this time in your life? Is there something you are trying to accomplish? Are you renovating your home or restructuring your business? Are you developing a relationship with someone—or a better relationship with yourself? Are you resolving a conflict? Perhaps you are seeking happiness or peace of mind or trying to be more loving. Perhaps you want to improve your health. Perhaps on reflection you realize that you want to spend more time with your child. Maybe you want to help others, but you feel blocked, so you do nothing. Perhaps you feel disconnected from others or yourself.

Notice if there are positive qualities you are not connecting with. Perhaps you are experiencing a lack of energy or an inability to take action. Do you lack inspiration? Are you unable to create or imagine or relate or speak or even feel? You may not even realize that you are carrying suppressed, untouched, or blocked emotions and feelings.

Notice the presence or absence of flow in your life, and if you feel confused or stuck, bring your attention to the stuck feeling. Locate this stuck energy in your body and breathe into it. Be with it. Take time to recognize where something in your life is not working, where you are feeling blocked, where you are not connecting, where you are not able to communicate. Are you aware of experiencing fear, lack, or doubt? Are you aware of negative self-talk? Whether with words or images, are you holding on to a pain identity? Are you aware of experiences or memories that are complex and have not been fully digested or integrated into your life?

Recognizing your pain or fear is essential in this practice, but that does not mean you need to analyze it. Rather, it means being in touch with how the pain or fear lives in you—how you see it and feel it. You could even have a conversation with it. You don't need to force awareness, however. Supported by the inner refuge, you can be aware of blockages without analyzing them. When you maintain connection with your experience as it is, difficult emotions and feelings will have the space to emerge.

Allow what you are feeling and connect with it. Giving space to your feelings is like being a loving mother who maintains a safe space in which her child can cry. She doesn't try to interfere with the child's frustration or sadness, or punish the child for expressing strong feelings. And because she simply holds the space for the child and allows its feelings to emerge, when the storm is over and the tantrum has released its energy, she discovers a child who is free and joyful. Providing the necessary protection and allowing the energy to move is critical. This is what the inner refuge provides when we feel stuck. Healing happens when we hold that space with awareness and allow ourselves to feel.

Maybe you already have a good sense of something within you that needs to be felt, expressed, and released. As you open to these blocked or repressed feelings, pay close attention to them. Recognize them, become familiar with them, get to know them intimately. As you connect deeply with the feelings, do you feel the need to move, to make a sound, to draw or write? Perhaps you feel an urge to paint, make music, sculpt, cook, or sew. My advice is: *Don't rush this process.* Stay with what you are feeling—talk to it, give it a voice, find out how it wants to be expressed. Instead of moving immediately into action, sit with your disappointment, your sadness, your anger. Connect with your emotional energies in the sacred space and listen.

Sometimes suppressed emotions are blocked in a specific part of the body. In that case, you could release those emotions by dancing with them or expressing them through some other form of movement. If the emotions are suppressed energetically, you could release them with your breath. Or you could sing or sound them in the safety of the refuge. Perhaps you need to unblock emotions through an expression of the mind. If, for example, you are trying to paint from an image or idea or memory that holds an emotional charge, you could connect with stillness, silence, and spaciousness until the emotions start to move. The emotions can then be channeled through the brush and paint onto the canvas and come out in a colorful artwork.

Whether you release blocked emotions through your body, speech, or mind, you are expressing the emotional energy creatively. And with that expression, you may feel *Wow, what a release, what freedom, what liberation!* That feeling of liberation is a taste of nirvana. Through your expression you have separated from the impure self and connected with the pure self that has been obscured. The self you don't want is now on the canvas or the page; the self you want is saying *Wow!* As one self leaves, the other is waiting to be encountered. You can feel all this inside you. The pure self, the self you have missed, is waiting for you to meet it. Separating ego from your true being, samsara from nirvana, is the benefit of rushen expression.

Through rushen art, every expression of sadness or pain becomes sacred art if it is expressed from the inner refuge. There is an important distinction to be made between sacred art and ordinary art. If you try to practice rushen art from a place other than the inner refuge, your agitated ego will be in charge, which means no stillness. You will have many confused voices guiding you, so no silence. And you will have a very limited idea of the work, so no spaciousness.

There are artists who are not grounded or balanced in their expression. They may have gone to art school, studied art history, and developed facility with technique, but they have no experience in making sacred art. I see some art pieces that make me wonder if their execution helped the artist. But if inspiration comes from the source, its expression will be transformative and can take the artist to a new place. We need to be careful not to make art solely out of our agitation, confusion, contraction, and limitation—the place of pure ego. The ground of sacred art is our connection to the spaciousness of being, the light of awareness, and the warmth of compassion—the inner refuge.

Rushen expression is a powerful way of doing art-work. Through this process, you are able to heal inner wounds, release blockages, and free yourself from what-ever frozen emotions and thoughts have imprisoned you. The benefit of rushen practice is that it separates negative emotion from positive qualities, a sense of disconnection from connection, ignorance from realization. Like any deep, therapeutic work, rushen practice disentangles the clear self from the unclear self, allowing you to find your clearer self through the practice of art. Eventually, when your artwork is consistently connected to the inner ref-uge, rushen practice will be a way to find not just your clearer self but your true self. At that point, your practice becomes tögel art.

Tögel art practice

While rushen art allows us to clear the impure self and connect with the pure self, tögel art expresses the pure self directly. Through expression, the pure self comes alive for you, for others, and for the benefit of all beings.

Sacred art practice may involve both rushen and tögel. You don't need to think of them as two separate practices. For example, if you are working with a deeply suppressed fear, you first connect with the three doors of stillness, silence, and spaciousness. Then, as you feel the support of the inner refuge, you allow the fear to surface and you meet it nakedly. As the fear emerges, you begin expressing it through whatever form you have chosen. This is rushen practice. As the fear moves into expression, you begin to feel free. You have a taste of feeling liberated. Tasting liberation in this way gives birth to confidence. This is not confidence in a conventional sense. It is con-fidence in the liveliness of being. You are alive and fully present. As you continue to experience spaciousness and awareness, you express that liveliness as tögel art. Separating fear from confidence in rushen art, you then express that confidence in tögel art. In this way, rushen art and tögel art flow together as one unbroken, ongoing journey.

Confidence is not the only quality you discover in the process of making tögel art. Positive qualities like love, joy, compassion, equanimity, openness, generosity, strength, and power also emerge. As the qualities you discover through rushen practice and tögel practice come alive, they can be integrated into your life. They become part of your body, speech, mind, relationships, work, and service. In the past, you may have felt confidence to some degree, but it may not always have been available when you needed it. If confidence isn't given voice, a way to manifest, it can't change your life or the world or any situation you encounter. Tögel art brings forth your positive, perfected, enlightened qualities, and you feel full and vibrant. Your positive qualities are not hidden; they are alive in you and are being expressed.

The first stage of this work is to clear the blockages. You cannot discover love without clearing anger, for example. In the second stage of the work, you connect with an emerging positive quality and give it expression. Manifesting any of the positive qualities is the essence of tögel art. When you uncover joy, for example, I encourage you to express it in whatever form you are comfortable with. If writing is your skill, let it be the path to express your joy. If you are a dancer, let that be your way. If conflict resolution is your profession, your work of art might be finding new ways to bring people together to resolve disagreements. Every positive expression can be transformative, bringing benefit to you and others.

The willingness to express is in itself a liberating experience. But you need to be flexible about the particular way in which you express. You might think, *I've had a problem with my mother for years, but I'm feeling love now and looking forward to expressing it to her.* That is a nice impulse, but if behind that voice is the thought, *This time my mother will be receptive to me, and she won't be so critical,* you are not open. You may decide to go ahead and express love to her anyway, but be aware that you have expectations and that the result might be painful if she does not respond in the way you want.

Similarly, in creating a piece of art, it is important not to have fixed ideas. Don't assume that the dance you found liberating 20 years ago will have the same effect today. It is not the product that makes sacred art. It is the artist and the process by which the artist produces the art that makes it an expression of enlightened qualities. It is important not to be too goal-oriented in your process and demand that the result be exactly this or that. The more you connect with openness, awareness, and warmth, the more authentic your expression will be. If you fix on a single outcome, it will be hard to find a satisfactory resolution. Be open to finding multiple possibilities. You are on a spiritual path and so many things can happen. Be flexible and see how things go. Be open to being surprised by the outcome of your practice.

Though rushen art and tögel art form a single process, there may be times when you can't make the transition from rushen practice to tögel practice. When your ego, your grasping mind, is very strong, it may intrude, fearful of making a mistake, of not doing a good job. Or you may be fixated on the outcome, thereby losing the freshness of the present moment. When that happens, it means you are not connected to the inner refuge—spaciousness, awareness, and warmth. If you try to make art when you are not connected, the ego will interfere. Whenever you feel that the ego is trying to take charge, take one of the precious pills—stillness, silence, or spaciousness—before resuming the process of making art.

Creative blocks

What if you feel blocked in your creative expression? What if you don't know what to say or write or sing? If there is no inner space, creativity will not flow. But when there is flow, inspiration may surprise you; it's like finding a treasure.

Whatever blockages we uncover in ourselves, we can see the power of hosting them. Anger, for one, cannot sustain itself without the person who is angry. In the deep refuge, the angry self does not exist; therefore, anger cannot be sustained. When you experience sacred space in the absence of anger, you feel inner light, warmth, and comforting presence, and love for the whole world. That feeling encourages you to be creative. Expressing inner light illuminates the darkness within you and touches others. This expression becomes what is known as bodhisattva activity in the world. A bodhisattva is one who aspires to bring healing and benefit to all beings.

When you are blocked, you can turn to the sacred syllables *A OM HUNG RAM DZA* to unlock the creative potential at each chakra. Singing a syllable while focusing your attention at the corresponding chakra activates the energy of that center and supports you in opening to blockages, allowing them to release. Singing *A* again and again while resting your attention at the crown, you experience the power of openness. Singing *OM* again and again while resting your focus at the throat chakra connects you with awareness of unlimited potential. Singing *HUNG* again and again while resting your attention at the heart chakra ignites the fire of inspiration. Singing *RAM* again and again while resting your attention at the navel chakra supports readiness—an attitude of *Let's do it!* And singing *DZA* again and again while resting your focus at the secret chakra propels you into action.

Positive qualities emerge, and from feeling blocked, you move into feeling their presence in your life. Imagination is activated; words and ideas flow. There is liveliness in your body. When a quality is active and alive, it doesn't matter what form your expression takes; let it flow. When you are open and aware and positive qualities ripen in you, actions are effortless. Effortlessness is a hallmark of sacred art.

Sacred art is not sacred because it looks beautiful— though it might—but because it emerges from unbounded sacred space and reflects the qualities of the inner refuge. Sacred art has a pure, spacious quality; it is full of light, awareness, clarity, and joy. Every piece of art captures a moment of being or embodies a way of living. Even an awkward expression can be sacred if your intention is pure. Maybe what you express doesn't make complete sense because it wasn't articulated clearly, but if there is openness and warmth in your expression, the sacred quality is there. Conversely, your creation may be beautiful and executed masterfully, but if there is no openness and warmth, the sacredness is missing.

Meditation:
Supporting rushen and tögel art

Sit in a comfortable position with your spine upright and your chest open. Take time to settle.

Connect with the three precious pills: stillness of body, silence of speech, spaciousness of mind. Allow time to connect.

Bring your attention to the crown of your head and then slowly move down the core of your body, resting your attention at each chakra. Inhale a few full, deep, fresh breaths at each location. As you move down the core of your body from chakra to chakra, allow each exhalation to support you in releasing any tension, anxiety, or agenda you are bringing to this moment.

Next, allow your attention to pervade your whole body. Rest in the stillness, silence, and spaciousness of being. Feel permission to just be.

Now reflect on an obstacle to expression that you may be experiencing in your life. As you connect with the blockage, notice any tension in your body, any internal chatter, or any other resistance or obstacle to expression. Become aware of stories or images that may be occupying you.

Again, starting at your crown, bring your attention to each chakra in succession. As you rest your attention at each energy center, notice how you experience the blockage there. Sing the corresponding syllable for that chakra three or more times. At the crown, sing A; at the throat, OM; at the heart, HUNG; at the navel, RAM; at the secret chakra, DZA. Let the sound move through you and any blockage you feel. Rest your attention in the fullness of your experience before moving on to the next chakra.

Become aware of the space that opens up at each chakra. Rest in the freshness there. Notice any quality that becomes available. Is joy available? Confidence? The vibration of each syllable you sing supports release of the blocked energy, awareness of a fresh sense of spaciousness, and the emergence of positive qualities.

As you connect with a quality that emerges, your awareness matures and ripens it. Remain aware of the positive quality as you continue to meditate.

Rest in the richness of the quality as long as your experience is fresh.

Dedicate the merit of your practice with the aspiration: *In liberating my own being, may I benefit others.*

In this meditation, you become familiar with the process of hosting a blockage in open awareness. Meeting and releasing the energy or emotion that is blocked is the essence of rushen practice. As you notice the freshness that becomes available, your continued awareness nurtures the positive quality that emerges. Expressing that quality benefits you and others. This is the essence of tögel practice.

Awakening inspiration

The way you connect with the fundamental space of being in tögel practice shifts your reality. The world no longer appears to be for you or against you. When your connection to being is stable, you see without disconnecting from yourself, speak without disconnecting, and move without disconnecting. You see what is. And what is, is always perfect.

The following meditation supports you in seeing the perfection in all things.

Meditation: Pure vision of openness, awareness, and warmth

Close your eyes and turn your attention inward. Become aware of stillness, silence, and spaciousness. Allow time to settle.

Rest in the stillness of being, silence of being, and spaciousness of being.

Now bring your attention to your heart. Connect with the sacred space in and around your heart. Feel the liveliness of awareness. Feel the warmth of presence. Abide here. Abiding in the vibrancy of your heart is medicine.

Imagine subtle channels of light connecting your heart to your eyes. Feel the sacred space, awareness, and warmth from your heart move upward to your eyes. Without losing your connection to spaciousness, awareness, and warmth, be aware of that inner movement. Rest here, feeling the vibrancy.

Now open your eyes. Feel the vibrancy moving through your eyes, illuminating everything you perceive. See the vividness in the world around you. Abide here.

Repeat this process beginning with the vibrancy in your heart, only now when you open your eyes, imagine you are seeing someone who has caused you pain. Can you experience the sacred in the other?

The other is the sacred space. The other is the light of awareness. The other is the warmth of connection. At this moment, you are seeing the sacred source in the other. You are seeing the light in the darkness. You are seeing the sacred in matter.

Dedicate the merit of your practice with the aspiration: *In liberating my own being, may I benefit others.*

This practice makes the connection between stillness and action, silence and speech, mind and form. It supports sacred manifestation by changing the reality you experience. When we speak about changing reality we first have to ask, *What is reality?* We know by now that what we perceive is not solid or fixed; it is constantly changing. And when we perceive the impermanence of our sense of self, it is transformative. Look at your partner, your neighbor, a stranger, or the natural world. Now observe yourself. What do you experience? Don't be too analytical about this. Just shift your attention and become aware of yourself in that moment. It is far more powerful to look at yourself than to fix your attention on another, because how you perceive yourself determines how you perceive others. When you are able to rest in the dynamic space of being, the circumstances around you can change and people can express in a variety of ways without affecting your stability.

By contrast, when you disconnect from the fundamental, unchanging space of being, you will project insecurity onto whatever appears. Your reaction will be based on how you experience yourself. When you are connected to the fundamental space of being, you experience life in a different way than your pain identity would. As strong as the evidence is that the self is ever changing, we often don't embrace that view. Instead, we constantly try to secure our experience of a solid self. We are unsuccessful in this, because we are not bringing our attention to the right place in order to perceive the stillness of being, silence of being, spaciousness of being. When we become familiar with the inherent stability of the inner refuge, what we do, say, and perceive doesn't separate us from the refuge.

The result of discovering the sacred space that abides in the heart, moves in the channels, and appears in objects is that we see beauty in everything and everyone. We experience nothing but the three perfect dimensions of spaciousness, awareness, and the vibrancy of qualities. We see space, light, and warmth everywhere. In the Bön and Buddhist traditions this is known as the appearance of the three kayas: the *dharmakaya*, or body of emptiness; the *sambhogakaya*, or body of light; and the *nirmanakaya*, or body of great bliss. Through the three doors of body, speech, and mind, we can experience these three pure dimensions of existence.

In suffering, however, we are more familiar with the opposite of these dimensions. We fixate on what is wrong or flawed and create a sense of self that is constellated around our suffering. We experience the world as an expression of our conflict and pain. We may have incredible experiences of openness and joy, yet continue to dwell on what disturbs us. The pure vision practice allows us to shift our allegiance from creating a continuity of suffering to discovering the continuity of wakefulness. We bring our attention to the base or ground of openness, awareness, and warmth in the heart and abide there. When we are stable in our connection to this ground of being, movement does not affect our stability. We move, but we are not disconnected from the fundamental, unmoving space of being. We see, but seeing does not affect our connection to the openness, awareness, and warmth of being.

One place you might experience seeing the sacred in another is in falling in love. Initially you see the other person as amazing. As you spend time with your lover, the world seems open and fresh and full of possibilities. So isn't it interesting that the very same amazing person can become such a disappointment when your vision changes? How is it possible that you can move from the beauty you saw initially to what you are seeing now? You come up with reasons: disappointments, hurts. But fundamentally the shift happened because you lost your connection to the openness of your heart. If you hadn't lost the connection, you probably would still be enough in love to continue appreciating your lover.

When we perceive something as being "out there," we don't realize its connection to our heart space. Appearances cause us to lose this connection to ourselves. We practice the pure vision meditation to connect with the openness of being by resting in the heart space, then moving to the eyes, and then to the world around us as it appears. As we remain connected to the openness of the heart, to the beauty and love and joy within our natural mind, we see that goodness reflected in the world around us. We experience the power of awareness to change our reality.

I encourage you to explore this in how you experience your family and close friends, your work environment, and the natural world. See how you can change a situation not through your actions but through a shift in your perception. In this way you will discover how joy can arise in the midst of suffering and hope can emerge in hopeless places, and how the spontaneous arising of openness, clarity, and creative energy can help others and change the world.

NYINGJE—Compassion

Chapter 5

Enlightened Service and Leadership

In my life as a monk, and later as a teacher, husband, and father, I have had many opportunities to serve others and be in a position of leadership. Bringing these activities to the path of dharma, to seeing all of existence and all of our actions as sacred, is core to the teachings I have received and the meditation practices I do and share with others.

At the heart of these teachings are two essential points: We need to minimize ego and maximize compassion. We need to be conscious when our actions arise from personal pain or conflict, and when they do, stop and find a more open space from which to act. We do not need to continue to act from pain. Sometimes we get caught up in reacting to a perceived injustice, or enmeshed in a conflict between people or arguing factions within a group. As we awaken to the way this conflict lives in us we can come to a clearer and more open place, and from there we can contribute positively to the situation.

As we continue through life, we are presented with more and more opportunities to serve others. Many of us take on roles of responsibility, whether through caring for children or aging parents, or taking up leadership positions in our jobs or communities. For those on a spiritual path, as we hear teachings, reflect on their meaning in our lives, and practice meditation, our motivation to help others increases. According to dzogchen, to attain spiritual maturity, it is not enough to realize your natural mind; you need to integrate this realization with your everyday experience. And it is not enough to integrate this with everyday experience; you need to give birth to positive qualities. Finally, it is not enough to give birth to positive qualities; you need to develop the means to express them for the welfare of others.

Being motivated to help others is not just a characteristic of people following a spiritual path; compassion is inherent in human nature. A mother wants to be a good mother; a husband wants to be a good partner; a child wants everyone around her to be happy. At a very basic level, it feels good to help others, whether you are helping an individual, a family, or a community.

If we reflect on our lives, we come to realize how much our actions affect one another. We are interconnected with all of life, and we begin to see the consequences of our individual and collective actions. How can we live in harmony with others and our environment and increase our capacity to benefit them?

The ultimate goal on the path of dharma is enlightenment—complete liberation from the suffering of existence. And when service becomes a sacred path, it too has that larger goal. In order for serving others to become a sacred path, our actions must come from two core realizations: selflessness and compassion.

Selflessness and serving others with compassion lead to liberation from suffering. Just as two wings of a bird are necessary for flight, selflessness and compassion are necessary for enlightenment.

The wisdom of selflessness

Selflessness is key to service as a spiritual path. Right now, at this moment in your life, what is your relationship to yourself? Are you trying to work with yourself, connect with yourself, find yourself? What is your relationship to those close to you? Are you trying to help a child, an elderly parent, a partner, a friend? What is your relationship to the wider world? Are you acting to benefit your community, trying to bring positive energy to your workplace, or dedicating yourself to protecting the environment?

Bring to mind a situation in which you are trying to help someone. Perhaps you face challenges to your efforts, and you are feeling frustration, disappointment, anger, or hopelessness. Whatever you are experiencing, recognize it in this moment without criticizing or judging it. Simply be conscious of what is happening when your intention is to help another. As you allow your experience to form in your imagination and you open to what comes to mind without judgment, turn your attention back to yourself and look more closely. Who is feeling challenged? Who is upset and angry? Who is tired or burdened? Who feels unacknowledged? Looking more deeply within yourself, you may discover fear or doubt or insecurity. When you face these challenges, it is important to recognize the pain identity, the sense of self that is associated with feelings like fear, doubt, or anger.

If you are looking at a situation through the eyes of a pain identity, even if your intention is to help and to serve, your actions are unlikely to bring positive results. In order to be effective, you first have to acknowledge that identity of fear or pain—the ego. Then you can explore minimizing the ego. Loosening the grip of the ego, the pain identity, does not mean getting rid of yourself. It actually means finding yourself. The true self is like water: It adapts to the shape of the vessel, the situation. But when your sense of self is bound and rigid, it doesn't change shape easily, and conflict with others inevitably ensues.

How can you find that sense of self that is open and sees potential and possibility in any situation? When you recognize that you are stuck and are experiencing a pain identity, rest your attention directly on this stuck experience of yourself. Resting your attention is the key. This is not the kind of attention that is panicking and trying to get rid of something, or trying to improve something, or even trying to analyze something and figure it out. Resting attention is open attention. It means being fully present with your experience. There is a natural feeling of warmth and generosity that comes with open attention. You can explore this by focusing directly on an experience of discomfort or confusion. Your focus is like a beam of light that illuminates the discomfort. If your mind starts to move into analyzing or judging, redirect your attention to simply being present with the discomfort. See it, feel it, be with it. Slowly, the object of your focus will change. Your discomfort may actually dissipate, because any painful sense of self needs to be maintained in order to exist. When you are fully present with your insecurity in the moment, it gradually becomes less substantial and releases. When this release happens, you glimpse openness. It is important to recognize and value this openness. You value it by resting your attention in the experience of openness. This is a glimpse of selflessness, a moment of discovering a sacred space within you where you are totally free.

While you may have experienced this space, it might not have been pointed out as significant. Or you might not have known how to maintain the experience, so it was not stable within you. When you are able to be present with your sense of self and your experience without analyzing or criticizing, any constricted sense of self releases, revealing a spaciousness of being that is not bound or confused. The unbounded spaciousness of being, even if experienced only momentarily, is sacred. From that unbounded sacred space, you come alive and can act in a beneficial way.

Once you recognize this sacred space, you are able to show up fully for yourself even when you feel the most uncertain or shaky. One glimpse of the sacred space gives rise to an entire path of living your life from the creative and open source of your natural mind. You begin to see again and again that any sense of yourself as solid and fixed isn't accurate or true, and any attempt to find or make yourself solid or fixed is misguided and unnecessary. Not only is this realization a relief, it is a joyful experience. The recognition of selflessness is the dawn of wisdom.

The recognition of selflessness is a direct perception; the searching mind cannot discover it. According to the teachings, you cannot find it if you are searching for it because this wisdom is so close. If you are directly and nakedly aware in this very moment, no matter what is happening, you will discover the impermanent nature of both the problem and the problem maker—you. What emerges is the clear and open space of being that is sacred and pure and always has been.

As we have been exploring, meditation supports us in becoming more familiar with the openness of being and discovering the nature of mind, which is open, clear, and infinitely creative. Realizing the lack of a permanent or solid self is a liberating experience. You don't have to control other people or situations. You don't even have to control your own feelings or anticipate what might happen next. You can trust that stillness, silence, and spaciousness will fully support you in letting everything be as it is.

Wisdom means tapping into the openness of every moment. Can you trust that openness? Can you trust the opportunities that arise? Are you ready for the open moment that will enrich your life?

If you remain connected to this very moment of spaciousness, there are infinite possibilities. And according to the teachings of dzogchen, all positive qualities without exception will arise from that space. In the teachings, compassion is the single word that summarizes all positive qualities. Compassion is the ability to perceive the suffering of others and act for their benefit. But you will not experience compassion if you are not open. You have to see the inherent openness of your being in this moment, in each moment. Many times we don't see the openness and the possibilities that are available because we are occupied with an old story. So wisdom is being open to the newness of each moment.

Wisdom is essential to serving others because it allows you to bring every challenge to your path. There is no wrong moment to discover wisdom. It is right here, in the middle of your irritation or your strong opinion about the way things should be. The question is, are you willing and committed to recognizing, exploring, and overcoming your stuck places? Can you realize the workability of every moment and not give up, passively waiting for things to change or for others to change?

When you realize you are waiting for someone else to change before you reach out to them, instead bring your attention to the present moment, to your experience of yourself as the one who is waiting and expecting—and is miserable. If you hold the proper space for this pain identity and bring open attention to it without judgment, your experience of yourself will begin to release, and you will discover the clear and open space of the moment. Don't dismiss the importance of this clear and open space. It is not just the absence of your pain identity that you experience in this space; the openness is full of possibilities. Feeling this in yourself, you will begin to notice possibilities in others.

When doing service, a good question to ask yourself is: *Who is trying to help?* The aspiration to help another is pure, but often it is hijacked by a pain identity. Perhaps you are lonely and need a friend. Perhaps you want acknowledgment or power. It is important to be aware when your pain identity is influencing your actions so you can ensure that your actions are coming from openness rather than from hidden needs. Service is the wrong place to look for acknowledgment or power. We enter spiritual service not to feed the ego but to surrender it.

We start with good intentions. Can you recall your initial motivation to be a mother, a partner, an employee, an employer, or a volunteer? Is that intention still alive in you? Are you coming from the space of openness? It is difficult to maintain your inspiration and act from the right space with enthusiasm when you are stuck in a pain identity and don't know how to connect to yourself in a better way. Your pain then becomes the familiar place, more familiar than your inspiration. And when you act from the familiar place of your pain, you end up feeling depleted, needing to receive more than to give. When you feel unbalanced or drained, that is a sign to stop and open to your experience of discomfort. Host it. The warmth of your presence will allow the discomfort to release, and you will discover a more open space to act from.

How then do we stay open? There is a direct connection between stillness and openness. If you feel a little shaky or off balance, instead of *trying* to be open, just be still. That stillness allows agitation to settle. When your agitation settles, openness is there. You have a glimpse of freedom. And from there you can express and act with an open heart.

Inner freedom

Inner freedom comes from selflessness. When you are connected to the inner source of being, you are enriched by actions that ego would experience as a loss. Take positive regard, for example. Most of us want to be well thought of, and we are sensitive to not being well received. We may fear the criticism of others, or imagine painful scenes in which we are being judged. We may be more occupied with thoughts about ourselves than with expressing positive regard for another. But with inner freedom, we discover the joy of allowing others to shine.

Allowing someone else to express a good idea you had that you wanted to claim as your own can be a joyful experience. You gain the confidence to allow diverse opinions. Opening to others becomes more rewarding than remaining closed and judgmental. Our capacity to be generous manifests from selflessness. It becomes possible when we trust the openness of being.

In our desire to help others, if we discover that our natural wisdom is obscured by a pain identity, we can overcome this limitation with the support of the three precious pills. As the pain identity is recognized, embraced, and released, the sacred space within becomes available. Connecting with and trusting this sacred space allows generosity to flow. Our actions change from effortful to spontaneous and joyful.

Meditation:
Connecting with wisdom

Bring your attention inward. Rest your attention on the stillness of your body. Allow time to connect with the stillness of being.

Now draw your attention to inner silence. Rest in awareness of silence. Allow time to release the mind's tendency to engage in chatter. Settle into the support of silence.

Become aware of the spaciousness of your mind. Let the spaciousness support you to allow your thoughts and feelings without rejecting them or chasing after them. Fully rest in the openness of being.

Connect with your motivation to help or serve others. Being of service does not have to be a grand gesture, but can be any situation in which you want to help an individual, your family, your community, co-workers, or the environment. As you bring this situation to mind, notice any challenges you may be experiencing. Be aware of any changes in your body or breath as you reflect. Be aware of any discomfort you feel. Allow time for this experience.

Can you recognize and feel a pain identity, a sense of self that is experiencing difficulty and feels challenged? Who is the one feeling pain? Are you feeling burdened or drained? Are you feeling rejected or unappreciated? That painful experience of yourself needs your attention, your open, nonjudgmental awareness.

Can you offer your pain identity a spacious, luminous, warm hug? Remain in pure presence without judging the pain self or disconnecting from it. Open to the experience. Rest in spaciousness, fully connected and aware. Awareness is luminosity, and kindness toward your pain is warmth. Be open, connected, and warm to yourself just as you would to a dear friend who was in pain—not judging, just being there, being kind.

As you hold the pain identity in this way, it will come to occupy less and less of your being. Eventually you may feel that there is just openness. This space is sacred. Be aware of it. The awareness that recognizes sacred space is wisdom. Wisdom naturally arises with the dissolution of the pain identity. As you become familiar with sacred space, spontaneous, effortless, compassionate action arises. Compassionate action is creative and does not have just one face. It is not limited to being nice. It can be smiling or encouraging or powerful or even wrathful, but the medicine of compassion always comes from clear space.

Dedicate the merit of your practice with the aspiration: *In liberating my own being, may I benefit others.*

Whenever you bring your pain identity into a relationship or a project, it is difficult to be of benefit, because you have not taken care of your own needs. When you cannot recognize and reflect upon and host your own pain, it is difficult to serve others. Your pain interferes, leaving you no clear space from which to act. No clear space means there is no wisdom, and without wisdom there is no genuine compassion. Whenever a situation affects you, if you become conscious of a pain identity that is operating and you can embrace it and then let it go in sacred space, that is wisdom. When the challenging situation is no longer driving you, your life becomes a meditation. Whatever you do becomes spiritual practice. As you open more to your own pain, you will become more aware of others' pain. Rich with spaciousness, you will naturally respect others and care for them.

Compassion

With wisdom we discover inner freedom, with compassion we act for the benefit of others. Having compassion for your children, husband, wife, colleague, boss, or anyone else you encounter improves the quality of your everyday life and makes it your spiritual practice. Many religions teach that we should have compassion for others, particularly the underprivileged and underserved. We are taught to place the welfare of others before our own. But often in our efforts to apply this spiritual advice we suffer. We suffer in trying to be nice. We suffer in trying to help others. Doing the right thing can be stressful when our kindness is not coming from the right place.

When our effort to be kind overrides the fear and old wounds we carry, when a hidden pain identity is ignored in the name of serving someone else, our actions are coming from the wrong place. We try so hard to be nice, while inside we are suffering. That is not genuine compassion practice; it is self-neglect. We abandon ourselves in the process of dedicating ourselves to serving others. In neglecting ourselves while serving others, we may build resentment: *Where is* my *acknowledgment? What thanks do* I *get? When do* I *get to take a break?* We may carry subtle expectations of others to meet our bypassed needs.

Another block to compassionate action is thinking that others need to change. When we take this conclusion for granted, this view goes unexamined. As a result, the dynamic possibility of our relationships is lost to us. Ego depends on seeing others as separate from us. When you find yourself thinking or wishing another would change, that is a manifestation of ego's separateness. So at this point stop and turn your attention inward to stillness, silence, and spaciousness. Stay present until you settle and begin to connect with a feeling of well-being. Now become aware of wanting the other to change. What is the quality you wish they would develop? Can you find that quality in yourself at this moment? As you connect with this quality, feel it throughout your entire body, and then imagine it moving into the world, in particular to support those you think should change. If you wake up to the quality in yourself that you wish others would possess, you will bridge the divide between you and them. As you embody the quality you want others to realize, you will become a positive agent of change.

In Buddhism, compassion begins with sympathy or empathy toward the suffering of others and a genuine motivation to help them be free from suffering. Having deep empathy for others' suffering while holding a clear wish for them to be free of it is a specific state of mind. You are aware of others' pain; you know how it feels. That is empathy, and it is a necessary step toward compassion. But compassion is more than empathy. It includes not only the wish that others be free from suffering but also the drive to act for their benefit.

Compassionate motivation is essential in leadership, but it is not always present. Leaders often limit their concern to their team or company or neighborhood or city to the exclusion of others. But we need to recognize how we limit our focus to our own pain and needs and conflicts, and explore expanding beyond our boundaries. Inclusion is the important direction in our maturation as compassionate beings. With the practice of compassion, we bring awareness to the suffering and the needs of others, and embrace a collective purpose or mission beyond our individual desires. Compassion teaches us how to break free of our conditions and attend to others. It plays an essential role in service and leadership.

A good leader creates a warm and open space in which to give others a voice, a space that can host diverse ideas, even conflicts, and allow their full expression. When we are able to offer that space to others, their creative and positive qualities emerge, and right action and collective decisions will result. When leadership is based on a compassionate and warm space for all, whether in a family, a classroom, a corporation, or a nation, the outcome is likely to have greater collective benefit. Good leadership is a genuine collaboration in which you feel a connection to others and to yourself. When you are leading a team doing a collective task, if you lack a harmonious connection, it will be harder to achieve your goal.

But what if you don't feel compassionate? How can you generate compassion? First, be aware of others. Pay attention to them. Think of people you are close to in your life, people you have an intimate relationship with or you are working closely with. Do you focus on their needs or only on your own? If you are in an intimate relationship, you might be preoccupied with your own insecurity: *How long will this relationship last? Is this person really interested in me? Why is this person not listening to me?* To awaken feelings of compassion, shift your concern to the other person. Think of their fears, their needs, their doubts, their insecurities, their inspiration, their joy. Just for a moment forget about yourself and reflect on the other.

So, to practice compassion, we shift our attention from self to others. Consider a situation in which you are helping others, whether you are working in a community garden, helping aging parents move into assisted living, or listening to a friend in distress. Look closely at how you engage with people when you are motivated to be of service. Notice where your actions are effortless. Notice where you are struggling. Do you experience any joy in serving others? The less your pain is involved in a situation the freer you will be to serve with ease and flow and playfulness.

The freer you are, the more readily you can recognize and draw on the resources that exist within you and the community. Whenever a collective—a family, a neighborhood, a community—faces a challenge and you as a member of the group can hold the challenge in open awareness, the intelligence of the collective will spontaneously give rise to solutions. No one person needs to carry the burden for all. What is needed is openness and an awareness of the collective space. By reflecting and being aware of your pain identity and hosting it in open awareness and the warmth of compassion, your pain releases and the openness you experience becomes a valuable resource for the whole community.

Meditation:
Opening to compassion

Find a posture that allows you to sit comfortably with your spine upright and chest open.

Just as a stuffy room benefits from opening a window to let in fresh air, you will benefit from taking a few deep, cleansing breaths. Breathe in deeply and hold your breath for a moment, then release it slowly. Do this three to five times as you settle into your posture.

Now rest your attention on the stillness of your body. Listen, hear, and feel the silence within and around you. Connect with a sense of openness throughout your body. Allow your body to rest in stillness, your voice to rest in silence, your mind to rest in openness. Rest in open awareness.

Gradually bring to mind people close to you who are facing challenges. That might be your aging parents, growing children, or friends experiencing illness, change, or loss. Pay closer attention to a particular relationship in which you are moved by the suffering of the other. Notice how the suffering of that person lives in your body, emotions, or mind. As you experience another's pain, stress, and discomfort, allow yourself to be supported by stillness, silence, and spaciousness. Be with your experience fully. Allow the warmth of empathy to be present.

Now broaden your focus to the wider world and those in difficult situations. If you are involved in community service or a collective challenge in your profession, bring to awareness those you are trying to serve. Notice how your body, breath, and mind are affected as you host collective suffering. Be aware of the support of stillness, silence, and spaciousness as you see, feel, and open to the pain of others. When you feel that support, empathy will naturally arise in the presence of suffering.

With the warmth of empathy, hold the intention: *May they be free from suffering.* Rest in your experience as long as it is fresh.

Dedicate the merit of your practice with the aspiration: *In liberating my own being, may I benefit others.*

In feeling the pain of others and allowing the experience of empathy, you cultivate compassion. As you find inner support, enabling you to open more and more to the challenges you experience in working with other people, you will feel a greater capacity to be present to their suffering. At any moment, you can move from a limited focus to a more inclusive, even global one. Take time to explore this simple shift of focus, and you will discover a deeper capacity for compassion.

But what happens if you become overwhelmed by the amount of suffering you perceive? Rather than shutting down or turning away, find the support that the three precious pills can offer on the spot. Become aware of the stillness of your body and rest your focus there. Become aware of the silence of inner speech and rest there. Become aware of the spaciousness of mind and rest there. Stillness will open to an experience of spaciousness that is inclusive. The experience of silence will open to awareness that is illuminating and free of judgment. The awareness of spaciousness can open your heart and allow the warmth of compassion to naturally arise. Being fully present with yourself and your experience will enable you to be part of the solution. You can take the three precious pills as many times a day as necessary. Pausing frequently for as little as 30 seconds throughout a busy day can bring a vital shift benefiting you and others.

While compassion is focused on the welfare of others, this does not mean that *you* do not benefit in serving them. A healthy focus on others is a way of helping yourself. Expressing your positive qualities gives vitality to your life.

Inspiring others to serve

An important aspect of enlightened leadership is inspiring other people to serve. Whether you are helping individuals or a community or larger society, any collective endeavor is almost impossible to accomplish without making others a part of it.

The first step is to have a clear intention, a purpose that is a collective vision or mission. This is a helpful reminder when challenges and conflicts arise. You can stop and host any challenge with warmth and presence, reconnecting with the collective vision for inspiration.

Working with other people is always about making a heart-to-heart connection. If there is no genuine connection, you cannot inspire others to collaborate in a way that supports collective creativity to emerge. So how can you bring out the best in others? When you doubt people, you undermine their ability to perform effectively. When you trust them, they begin to be more trustworthy. To trust others you need to let go of your attachment to how things should work.

When others are inspired, they are likely to be creative and take initiative. But are you threatened by their ideas? Do you feel they are taking something away from you? Connecting with the boundless source within you gives you the support to let go and let others contribute. People may be ready to join a collective endeavor, but you might be preventing them if your pain body, pain speech, or pain mind is activated. Look closely: Are you attracting people to serve? People need to feel openness and warmth from you.

Being open to others' participation also involves taking risks. Things may not work out as you envision, things may even go wrong, but if you are able to hold the space for the unexpected, your confidence will inspire the best in others. When you are playful and flexible, joy and creativity arise spontaneously.

At some point in serving others you may feel that your role is coming to an end. Is it time for you to step down from a leadership position or move into another area of service? Perhaps you are losing the internal qualities necessary to serve well. If it is time for others to assume leadership, are you open to that possibility? Is it a question of finding the right people? Do you need to be more trusting of others in order to let go? If you are genuinely open to change, the right people will appear. Make sure you are not creating an obstacle by holding on and not allowing space for others to enter.

Perhaps you need to open your view with *A* and connect to the field of possibilities with *OM*. If your vision of what is necessary is too fixed, it may block new directions and possibilities from emerging. Open your heart with

HUNG and allow a vision of others stepping forward to lead. With *RAM* you might reflect on your good fortune at having been able to serve and your desire to give others the same opportunity. If other people feel your openness, your enthusiasm, your joyful effort, your positive motivation, with *DZA* you open the door to allow their leadership qualities to emerge.

Wisdom is the discovery of freedom. In the realm of service and leadership, we need wisdom to free us from getting trapped in our own pain and ego. We need compassion to pay attention to others and care for them. We mature on our spiritual path when through wisdom we minimize ego and through service we maximize compassion. When you find and trust the support of the inner refuge, you can meet the challenges you face in living a fully connected life. You can liberate your pain identity and tap into the highest place in you. From there your creative and spontaneous actions will benefit others.

In my tradition, we recite prayers or wishes for the long life of our teachers, whom we deeply respect as a source of the teachings and as guides on the path to realization. Such a prayer was written for me by my own teacher, who responded to a request made by my students. The last line of this prayer is: *May your lifespan be perfectly fulfilled.* This refers to the complete expression of the positive qualities that awaken in you and bring benefit to others. So this is the aspiration I offer you:

May you fully realize your true nature. May your positive qualities emerge. May you honor your gifts by expressing them in your life. May others benefit from your presence in this world.

Index

C

D

L

M

T

Acknowledgments

I dedicate this book to all of my teachers, past and present, each one an example of the transformative power of spiritual practice. Their wisdom, grace, knowledge, and compassion empower all that I do, and I bow to each of them in gratitude for their many blessings.

I thank my wife, Khandro Tsering Wangmo. Tsering allows so much space for all the positive qualities to manifest in our life together. She is generous, caring, and supportive not only of our immediate family but also of our much larger spiritual family, extending all around the world. In my life, her openheartedness and joyfulness are like the clear blue sky.

This is my fourth book with Hay House and Patty Gift. Patty has once again shepherded me through the process of writing a book with her characteristic gentleness, ease, and professionalism. Anne Barthel, also of Hay House, and Joan Duncan Oliver edited the manuscript. Their care and diligence have much improved the work and made it both more readable and more readily accessible. Thank you.

Marcy Vaughn is the one person without whom this book could not exist. No one better understands how to communicate in writing my style of teaching. Thanks to Marcy, this book conveys the teachings in a clear, accessible, and authentic manner. Marcy is also the practice leader at many of my retreats in the United States, and leads retreats around the world for both Ligmincha and

The 3 Doors. From the depth of my heart, I am grateful to have such an extraordinary student and colleague.

Sue Davis Dill, Ligmincha's executive director, has supported me for 18 years. Over the years, she has held so many roles while helping support the Ligmincha sangha and me. Her administrative and organizational support even extends to helping me with my publication internationally. Thank you.

I express my gratitude to Rob Patzig and his wife, Eileen. Rob's work as president of the board of Ligmincha International frees me to teach more, write more, and create more. Eileen is his support, just as Tsering is mine.

I also extend my appreciation to all those who work on behalf of Ligmincha International and The 3 Doors. In liberating our own being, may we benefit others.

About the Author

A highly respected teacher and meditation master in the Bön Buddhist tradition, Tenzin Wangyal Rinpoche has students in over 25 countries around the world and reaches many more through his programs online. He is the founder and spiritual director of Ligmincha International, a nonprofit organization dedicated to preserving the ancient wisdom and culture of Tibet and sharing it in a way that is relevant to practitioners today. He is also the founder of The 3 Doors, an international nonprofit that teaches Tibetan meditation methods with practical applications for everyday life, and of Lishu Institute, a residential center in northern India for intensive study and practice of Bön. Tenzin Rinpoche is an acclaimed author, whose books include *Awakening the Sacred Body*, *Awakening the Luminous Mind*, *Tibetan Sound Healing*, and *The True Source of Healing*. He lives in northern California with his wife and son.

Links: ligmincha.org; the3doors.org; www.facebook.com/tenzinwangyalrinpoche

Hay House Titles of Related Interest

YOU CAN HEAL YOUR LIFE, the movie,
starring Louise Hay & Friends
(available as an online streaming video)
www.hayhouse.com/louise-movie

THE SHIFT, the movie,
starring Dr. Wayne W. Dyer
(available as an online streaming video)
www.hayhouse.com/the-shift-movie

*COMMIT TO SIT: Tools for Cultivating a Meditation Practice
from the Pages of Tricycle,* edited by Joan Duncan Oliver

QUANTUM CREATIVITY: Think Quantum, Be Creative,
by Amit Goswami, Ph.D.

*SECRETS OF MEDITATION, REVISED EDITION:
A Practical Guide to Inner Peace and
Personal Transformation,* by davidji

WHY MEDITATE? Working with Thoughts and Emotions,
by Matthieu Ricard

All of the above are available at your local bookstore,
or may be ordered by contacting Hay House (see next page).

We hope you enjoyed this Hay House book. If you'd like to receive our online catalog featuring additional information on Hay House books and products, or if you'd like to find out more about the Hay Foundation, please contact:

Hay House, Inc., P.O. Box 5100, Carlsbad, CA 92018-5100
(760) 431-7695 or (800) 654-5126
(760) 431-6948 (fax) or (800) 650-5115 (fax)
www.hayhouse.com® • www.hayfoundation.org

Published in Australia by: Hay House Australia Pty. Ltd.,
18/36 Ralph St., Alexandria NSW 2015
Phone: 612-9669-4299 • *Fax:* 612-9669-4144
www.hayhouse.com.au

Published in the United Kingdom by: Hay House UK, Ltd.,
The Sixth Floor, Watson House, 54 Baker Street, London W1U 7BU
Phone: +44 (0)20 3927 7290 • *Fax:* +44 (0)20 3927 7291
www.hayhouse.co.uk

Published in India by: Hay House Publishers India,
Muskaan Complex, Plot No. 3, B-2, Vasant Kunj, New Delhi 110 070
Phone: 91-11-4176-1620 • *Fax:* 91-11-4176-1630
www.hayhouse.co.in

Access New Knowledge.
Anytime. Anywhere.

Learn and evolve at your own pace
with the world's leading experts.

www.hayhouseU.com

Hay House Podcasts
Bring Fresh, Free Inspiration Each Week!

Hay House proudly offers a selection of life-changing audio content via our most popular podcasts!

Hay House Meditations Podcast

Features your favorite Hay House authors guiding you through meditations designed to help you relax and rejuvenate. Take their words into your soul and cruise through the week!

Dr. Wayne W. Dyer Podcast

Discover the timeless wisdom of Dr. Wayne W. Dyer, world-renowned spiritual teacher and affectionately known as "the father of motivation." Each week brings some of the best selections from the 10-year span of Dr. Dyer's talk show on Hay House Radio.

Hay House Podcast

Enjoy a selection of insightful and inspiring lectures from Hay House Live events, listen to some of the best moments from previous Hay House Radio episodes, and tune in for exclusive interviews and behind-the-scenes audio segments featuring leading experts in the fields of alternative health, self-development, intuitive medicine, success, and more! Get motivated to live your best life possible by subscribing to the free Hay House Podcast.

Find Hay House podcasts on iTunes, or visit www.HayHouse.com/podcasts for more info.